PRAISE FOR
BACKWOODS WITCHCRAFT

"Wander the ways of witchcraft in the mountains of Appalachia! In *Back-woods Witchcraft*, Jake Richards presents a fresh perspective on the practices, lore, and magick of the hillfolk of Tennessee. Jake offers a plethora of charming tales from his family and upbringing as the reader is delighted to partake in a time-honored, homegrown, century's-old culture of ritual, spells, and beliefs from the American South."

—CHRISTOPHER ORAPELLO, podcaster, artist,
and coauthor of *Besom, Stang & Sword*

"Jake has dug deep into the mountains and the land to share the wisdoms of his people, and he has done a wonderful job. He has shook the memory of this ole conjure woman and made me remember some things that I haven't thought of in years. I feel that this book is a blessing from the ancestors to draw forth knowledge that has been citified, changed, and lost. The land holds the memory, bones, and blood of the ancestors; and knowledge holds the key to unlocking what has been lost. I feel this book will help some to turn the key and open that door. Many blessings, Jake, and congratulations on a job well done!"

—from the foreword by STARR CASAS, author
of *Old Style Conjure*

"In *Backwoods Witchcraft*, Jake Richards shares his memories of growing up with Appalachian folk magic practices as they were passed on to him through generations within his family. In so doing, he offers a snapshot in time, recording and preserving a tradition of American folk practices, many of which are being forgotten in the post-industrial age. Richards presents family stories and experiences that came with learning the charms and formulas themselves. In doing so, he teaches the techniques in the context of the ideas behind the recipes, something that is often lacking in a lot of books on American folk magic. His writing comes across as humble, sincere, simple, and clear to follow. *Backwoods Witchcraft* is a great contribution to the writings on traditional folk magic."

—MAT AURYN, author of *Psychic Witch: A Metaphysical Guide to Meditation, Magick, and Manifestation*

BACKWOODS WITCHCRAFT

CONJURE & FOLK MAGIC FROM APPALACHIA

JAKE RICHARDS

FOREWORD BY STARR CASAS

WEISER BOOKS

This edition first published in 2019 by Weiser Books, an imprint of

Red Wheel/Weiser, LLC
With offices at:
65 Parker Street, Suite 7
Newburyport, MA 01950
www.redwheelweiser.com

Bible verses in the text are from the King James edition.

ISBN: 978-1-57863-653-2

Library of Congress Cataloging-in-Publication Data available upon request.

Cover design by Kathryn Sky-Peck
Cover photograph by BigStock / Moth art © Jake Richards
Interior by Maureen Forys, Happenstance Type-O-Rama
Typeset in Adobe Jenson Pro with Pinto and York Handwriting

Printed in Canada
MAR

10 9 8 7 6 5 4 3 2 1

I will lift up mine eyes unto the hills,
from whence cometh my help.
PSALM 121:1

CONTENTS

FOREWORD

When I was first asked to read Jake's book, I'll be honest, I didn't really know what to expect. I thought to myself, I'm gonna read it with an open mind and go from there. I have to say I wasn't expecting some of the things he has shared in this book. These are things you don't see written about or talked about—the only way you know about them is if you were raised in a family who told the stories and lived the life. There are tons of hidden wisdoms within the pages of this book. You simply have to know what you are looking at to find them.

There was a time before the internet when charms and works were thought of as nothing more than ole wives tales and backward folks' superstition. Things have changed, and now folks are beginning to see and to understand just how powerful those superstitions and wives tales really are; because at the end of the day, they aren't just tales after all, but a strong foundation that some of us are lucky enough to build upon. I feel like the ancestors are pushing forward, they want the wisdom of past ages shared. Folks need the powerful foundation of these ole tales in today's world, and Jake has done a wonderful job of sharing his knowledge through this book.

Some knowledge about this work has been worn thin by writers and folks who found it online; Jake shares information that I have never seen anyone reach or write about anywhere. For instance, I have never seen anyone talk about a corncob over the door for protection! I know that work because of how I was raised, but I'm sure this is new to some folks. The reason it is good for protection is because of all the holes in the cob—the work would have to find its way through all of them to get to the house. It's a very powerful work. Then there is the potato work he gives—once again, only someone raised on the stories would know this is not information that is widely known.

This book is filled with useful knowledge, and I feel even the oldest worker will benefit from it. Jake has dug deep into the mountains and the land to share the wisdoms of his people, and he has done a wonderful job. He has shook the memory of this ole conjure woman and made me remember some things that I haven't thought of in years. I feel that this book is a blessing from the ancestors to draw forth knowledge that has been citified, changed, and lost. The land holds the memory, bones, and blood of the ancestors; and knowledge holds the key to unlocking what has been lost. I feel this book will help some to turn the key and open that door. Many blessings, Jake, and congratulations on a job well done!

STARR CASAS, author of *Old Style Conjure*

ACKNOWLEDGMENTS

I would like to dedicate this work firstly to my mother, Brandi, for always being the one who held everything together and for taking on the world for us growing up. I owe all my strength to you. You were also the one who encouraged me to go down this path and complete this book. You made me believe in myself when you didn't think you could go on another day. Thank you for giving me a way to see.

To my grandmother Margaret for always being my best friend, my second mother, and my partner in crime. Your wisdom and love has deepened my life and spirit more than you will ever know.

To my late grandfather Eugene for always being the highest point, in my mind, of mountain faith. You had your battles, but you won out in the end. Must run in the family. Although today we would have differing views on things, I hope I've made you proud in some way.

To my late great-grandmother Lois thank you for showing me to always look for the top of the mountain, no matter how low the valley I'm in may be. I will always cherish your memory.

To my late grandfather John Critchton who sadly did not get to see my first publication through. Thank you for instilling in me some of the sense it takes to get through this world and the humor to go along with it.

To my partner, Torrey. You've been by my side through more things than most people can stand for. You've seen me at my worst and my best, and always loved and supported me either way in everything I do. I cherish you for that.

And lastly, to all our ancestors, known and unknown, who depended on this mountain work and medicine to survive. Your trials and troubles are seen, you are understood, and you are remembered.

PREFACE

Now, most folks have heard of the hoodoo and folk magic practiced in Louisiana, Texas, and other ways out west. But ours is rarely spoken of, if at all remembered. The witchcraft of these hills is a culmination of the practices of different tribes and peoples who settled in these mountains long ago—people who just mixed into the roots and rocks of the hillside and called it home. Now those roots and rocks are becoming a grave.

Nestled here in some of the oldest mountains on earth, our people are a mixed breed of the Irish, Scottish, German, and other settlers who came to call these hills home. This mixture includes the folk practices brought up through the slave trade and the practices learned by the neighboring indigenous tribes of the Cherokee, Creek, Shawnee, and Delaware. This craft speaks from the unmarked graves of slaves, old church bells, and broken pottery fragments of the Cherokee strewn about the creek bed. It is a remnant of our deep roots and a testimony of Appalachian life.

The hollers of North Carolina, the valleys of Virginia, and the mountains of Tennessee have been witness to a system of witchcraft unique among its sister traditions of the Deep South and cold North as well as its child tradition of the Ozarks. This craft has been passed down through whispers over biscuits in the kitchen, seen in the hands of grandmothers sewing or spinning wool while entranced, and smelled in the chimney smoke carried up the mountainside. It's in the digging by sore hands and the churning of the mortar and butter churn. It's work and a way of life.

You may have heard this craft called granny magic, hill folks hoodoo, or mountain conjure, but it's all the same. Every name describes the same rooted ways of my ancestors and the lands they chose to lay their bones in. The old folks didn't call it much of anything, really; but back then those who knew these ways were called healers, tellers of tales, power doctors, and conjure folk—and yarb doctors by the Christian townsfolk.

Today, we call these workings and beliefs a multitude of things: Appalachian folk magic, Appalachian conjure, or simply trying. All terms denote the same practice, but each worker prefers a particular one—or maybe none at all. But back then it was just what you did or said when you needed something. It wasn't magic or spells: it was life and prayer.

I grew up in East Tennessee in the valleys below Buffalo and Roan Mountain. My family was mostly farmers in Virginia, Tennessee, and North Carolina, some going back a good three hundred years. I spent most of my childhood at my great-grandmother's house on the side of Big Ridge Mountain near Devil's Nest in North Carolina. My family always spoke of the old wives' tales and folk remedies; who could cure what or what to do if this or that happened. They were mountain people to the bone: hunters, farmers, blacksmiths, faith healers, preachers, and root diggers.

My family's history is filled with this work. Papaw Oscar was a water witch. Papaw Trivett never met his daddy, so he could cure thrush, stop blood, and "blow out" burns. Mama's a seventh daughter, a natural-born healer. Nana has the sight and dreams true. And the list goes on.

Most of the knowledge of these hills has been lost to the oppressions of time and poverty. Before, this knowledge was known only by memory, and now the elders are quickly passing or forget. My mother's mother has forgotten due to the Alzheimer's, but she still sees. Young folks are walking around not knowing they have some of these gifts. We need a new generation to keep these roots alive. I am of that generation, and I hope you will be too. This magic is more than a tale of the hills and the whispers of the autumn fog; it's the history of my blood and bones, and possibly yours.

INTRODUCTION

THROUGH THE QUILTING HOOP

The unique thing about Appalachian folk magic is that there's no one right way to do it. Depending on what mountain or holler your family is from, you might practice differently. These differences are due, in part, to the close clans of the Irish and Scottish who came here. Maybe those traditions were unique to the clan and the region they came from. These were further separated by oral traditions being passed down through generations in different regions and evolving over time. The way I prepare candles and tie knots is different from the way my friends do in Virginia.

The common links between the formulas are the practices, beliefs, and good sense. Some families prefer to use candles for rituals, while others prefer oil lamps (this all depends on how many kids you have and how likely it is the light will get knocked down). Some families hang corncobs over the door for good luck, while others use horseshoes.

What I'm presenting in this book is what I have learned from my own family and gathered in my conversations with other mountain workers. You'll learn the ways we watch the smoke, charm the fire, and stir the water to tell fortune and fates. You'll see how we work the candles and lamps, cure unnatural illness, and jab those who do us wrong.

Appalachian folk magic is by no means a complete tradition. It varies by location, family, and time. Of course, all folk magic traditions in these Highlands are but fragments of history, like a line of camera film with missing frames or indiscernible images. This is an heirloom passed down of the oral traditions, broken in places and with pieces missing.

The works and ways you will find in this book are both new and old. The roots to them are true and worn, with add-ons here and there from my own learning and my own making that I have found to work. Any additions are crafted by the same thought and needs, tied with the same cord of prayers, and blessed by the same name. This book is a partial reconstruction of a continued way of living and surviving.

This is my attempt at piecing together the lost works and ways that were once practiced abundantly on this red clay earth while bringing them into today's mind and wonderings, with the seams fitted to the new shape and dimension of a modern societal framework. This is my offering to the past, to the history of these hills and the future survival of our twisted roots.

I will do my best to explain these ways in great detail for those new to the practice. I can also promise you that I do not sell lies or speak on that which I do not know. Those who know me know that I have a no-nonsense attitude when it comes to this work, and I will keep that same mind-set here. You will not find rehashed practices of Wicca or other traditions that have been told and sold as Appalachian more times than you can count.

Instead, I'll teach you the charms and roots of my family, in exchange for your promise to uphold this tradition and preserve it as it is and was and will be. I am the only yarb doctor on both sides of my family now who actively does this work. Help me bear the candle, light your flame from mine, and let's continue this for a thousand more generations to come.

Now, I also know that I tend to ramble a bit, going from one thing to another. For your sake, I will do my best to not pull you down other trails. No guarantees, though. Because how else do you learn the mountain if you don't get lost a bit?

THE BIBLE AND GOD

Regardless of your own preferences or beliefs, the Bible plays a major role in Appalachian folk magic, as it is set into the religious traditions of the Southern Baptists and Protestants. The Bible is often used as a "spell book" of sorts, but those who grew up in a close-knit Baptist household in Appalachia understand that the Bible means more than just the Word of God. It's the cinnamon candy at the bottom of Nana's purse. It's the sound of bells and the stiffness of church clothes on Sunday morning. It's the sweat and tears of decades of preaching and testifying. It's the soul of our people.

In Appalachia, the family Bible was often used to record births, deaths, marriages, and other events. Important dates and names would fill the blank pages inside, as would makeshift family trees, pictures, certificates, and newspaper clippings, and locks of baby hair or a baby's hospital bracelet. These Bibles are a testimony to the history of the people, written by the people. I have a couple of my grandfather's Bibles that I continue to use the way he did.

In my family, it wasn't so much as you're going to hell for not following its teachings. My father once said, "It just makes sense. All your ancestors were Christian." That's only somewhat correct, but what he meant hit me deeply. So, at least in my family, family tradition is as important as the Word of God, and they interconnect in many places.

With it being tradition, one would think the Bible was held to a high law, but it was actually followed quite loosely. Many folks will to this day get drunk on Saturday and go to church on Sunday to ask for forgiveness. These hills know the sins of its people, but they are understood. Christianity in Appalachia is a different flavor from the rest of the country—hell, the rest of the world. The harshness of biblical law was often softened by the oppressions dealt to Appalachian people. They were humble and isolated; alone except for the family on the mountain and the Man Upstairs. I presume God here became more of a parent than a king to be bowed to. He became company, family, and the refuge of these hills.

Aside from being heavenly law, the words of the King James Bible held power when spoken or written. The most famous verse here is the Blood Verse (Ezekiel 16:6), which is used to stop bleeding in man and beast alike:

> *And when I passed by thee, and saw thee polluted in*
> *thine own blood, I said unto thee when thou wast in thy*
> *blood, Live; yea, I said unto thee when thou wast in*
> *thy blood, Live.*

Nana often recited John 6:50 when baking bread ("This is the bread that comes down from heaven, so that one may eat of it and not die") and Joel 2:19 when cooking ("Yea, the LORD will answer and say unto his people, Behold, I will send you corn, and wine, and oil, and ye shall be satisfied therewith"). She'd also rub some lard or oil on her joints for arthritis while reciting Proverbs 16:24 ("Pleasant words are like a honeycomb, sweet to the soul and health to the bones).

My Papaw Trivett was a Baptist preacher who never met his father because he died early on. There was an old saying that held true with Papaw: a boy who had never met his father can cure thrush, burns, and bleeds. He could make a child cry and suck up their exhaled breath to cure colic, and he could blow on a burn to extinguish the "fire" left in it. But Papaw had a knack for many other things, too. He could remove a fever or illness by "running the egg"; he could wash warts off with a rag or bundle them up with a bag of stones. He was also one of the few men I've ever met who had "the sight," which in Appalachia is believed to appear more in the women of the family, as it did with my grandmothers, my mother, and my sister. The sight is seeing things before or as they happen; it's "talking to God," and it's "dreaming right." Papaw said it was his blessing from God, as did Nana. They knew everything and anything when it was gonna happen or if you were hiding something. Papaw said he wouldn't be here for that Christmas, and he wasn't. He passed away eight days prior.

Being influenced by Christianity may lead some to presume there's no harm done in this work. Far from it. Appalachian folk magic doesn't follow the Wiccan Rule of Three or the popular concept of karma. It goes by the biblical guidance, "an eye for an eye, and a tooth for a tooth." My grandmother was quick to get that beet juice when someone threatened the family or just did her plain wrong. As my family always said, "She'd curse you by the same name she blessed you." Any kind of curse or retaliation must be justified, and the punishment must fit the crime. If not, the scales will tip back on you since you created a larger imbalance than they. If the work is justified and fits the crime, the target can't get it removed until the spirits deem it over.

I use the Bible often in my craft because words have power and most verses are perfect for a number of things. For example, if you are doing a work for prosperity, you could recite Ezekiel 36:29–30:

> I will save you from all your uncleanness. I will call for the grain and make it plentiful and will not bring famine upon you. I will increase the fruit of the trees and the crops of the field, so that you will no longer suffer disgrace among the nations because of famine.

Or Proverbs 8:18–21:

> Riches and honor are with me, enduring wealth and righteousness. My fruit is better than gold, even fine gold, and my yield than choice silver. I walk in the way of righteousness, in the paths of justice, granting an inheritance to those who love me, and filling their treasuries.

For the old folks, the Bible also seems to have become a template for spells. Many spells still done today are fabricated and symbolic of biblical stories, especially in regard to the use of some animals. One such animal is the robin: it's believed that the robin's breast is red because it was stained with Christ's blood after pulling out the biggest thorn from His brow. Due to this folk story, robin eggs are cooked up to cure illnesses and get rid of curses, their feathers are luck bringers, and the sticks of their nest are said to keep the Devil away. This could also be connected to Deuteronomy 22:6–7:

> *If a bird's nest chance to be before thee in the way in any tree, or on the ground, whether they be young ones, or eggs, and the dam sitting upon the young, or upon the eggs, thou shalt not take the dam with the young: But thou shalt in any wise let the dam go, and take the young to thee; that it may be well with thee, and that thou mayest prolong thy days.*

Another animal-influenced formula was said to cure convulsions, rheumatism, fever, and a number of other ailments. The patient is to get seven hairs or clippings from the darker fur on a donkey's back (called the donkey's cross) and wear them in a flannel bag around their neck. (The old folks say that before Christ rode a donkey into the city of Jerusalem, it had an unmarked hide. The cross shows that it has been sanctified by the Savior. This, paired with the fact that Jesus specifically requested a donkey, creates the reasoning behind the donkey's cross and its miraculous power in healing. A donkey colt is sometimes recommended for this work, depending on family tradition and region, as the colt is a biblical symbol for meek obedience and peace.)

In the witch lore of Appalachia, one method for "becoming" a witch prescribes sprinkling dirt from the churchyard over a silver platter while renouncing Christ and saying the Lord's Prayer backward.

The person would then go down to the creek and state, "As Christ's blood washed away man's sin, so may this water wash me from Him." The platter is then dipped in the water and the dirt is washed off. In another, one was said to wait until midnight on a Friday and create a circle of flour on the floor in the kitchen. You were to crouch down in the center of it and read the last seven verses of Revelations backward. Then at the strike of midnight hold out your hand palm up, being silent the whole time. It was said then that the Devil would give you the power to "witch" or do anything you wanted to so long as you took offerings to him at the crossroads for seven years.

ANCESTOR WORK

The first step of this craft is to acknowledge your ancestors. My ancestors include those sold into slavery with chains around their necks and those made to walk the Trail of Tears, African and native alike. The Scotts-Irish were uprooted by adversity and poverty. Death and disease followed them, but they were accepted in these mountains and always will be. They endured torture and pain that would bring today's people to their knees. No human being deserves anything that was done to them. But look! My family and I are still here. That speaks to their perseverance and strength to survive.

Their wisdom and practices were often all these people had when they arrived. The slaves had nothing but the stories and songs of their land, and the Cherokee held on tightly to their spirits and knowledge of their elders. Many elders died coming to America or traveling along the Trail of Tears. This forced others to bear the weight of carrying the sacred through the world, often before their traditions would have normally allowed it.

These groups shared many things in common—things that were strong enough to outlive the differences of their culture and creed. All of them were broken and beaten down by oppression, treated like animals, but they kept their pride and hope. Today, we're true like the Irish, hardheaded like the Cherokee, and strong like the Africans.

Through this work, your ancestors will come to be your best aid, support, and protection. Most people treat ancestor work like it's a trade, a transaction: they help us, we give offerings, and that's that. Lord, if that ain't further from the truth. In this work you will meet ancestors who weren't very good in life, who bring to light the sins of your blood, and you will be faced with the task of healing these generational wounds. As a descendant of slave owners, slaves, natives, and Indian killers, I see the role I must take when it comes to my own blood.

My eighth great-grandfather, Frank Lytle, was born into slavery to his slave mother, Ester, and his master, Thomas Lytle. When Thomas died, Frank was granted his freedom. Discovering this information has changed my work with the ancestors profoundly. I now know I am a descendant of slaves and of slave owners, that I contain the blood of those who raped and murdered and of those who were raped and murdered. Many of you reading this are, too. So, we must ask ourselves how we can purify this blood and redeem it. What in your life can you do to atone for the sins of your blood? In our more recent past, we may see generational loops of absent fathers, addiction, and self-harm. We'll speak more on this later, but I want you to chew on these thoughts a little now.

Before we step foot into the magical practices of these hills, though, we're going to take a look at the tales of the Appalachian Mountains. As much as I'd like to be simple and straightforward, we must follow these threads and stories since most people have no clue what our practice is about or what soil it grows from. The same could be true for the folk practices of your region: just as intricate and tangled, refusing to be pulled from history's cold hands, needing someone to carry the torch.

Terrain often helps shape the culture and collective mind of a people. You have to understand the terrain and history of a people to see the reasons behind their thinking and ways when it comes to this odd tradition of witchcraft. For me, the dark trails on the mountain, hilltop graveyards at midnight, and an ever-present fear of the unknown were fertile ground for superstitions to take root and grow from the seeds of other lands. The bone-chilling call of cows at night and the owls hooting overhead instilled my people with a careful hand and conscious word so as not to tempt fate or death. Let me take you back to the Highlands of my ancestors, to the point where their magic was born. Come on, take a look through Mamaw's quilting hoop with me. Listen close and learn her stories.

1

THESE ROOTS RUN DEEP
Terrain and Culture in Appalachia

The Appalachian Mountain range, as it currently exists, begins at Belle Isle, just off the coast of Labrador north of Newfoundland in Canada, and stretches to Cheaha Mountain in Alabama. These hills are thought to be around 500 million years old. For some context, the Himalayas are just 40 million years old. This would make the Appalachian Mountains the second oldest mountain range in the world. So, more things have occurred in these hills than you could shake a stick at. What's left of living memory regarding the tales of this Highlands stands true to that as well. From the times of the old villages of the Cherokee to the Civil War battlefields where flesh met gun, history and superstition have always danced around each other.

The cultural boundaries of Appalachia are more so to the middle and southern regions of the mountain chain. The Appalachia that I know best spans five states: Tennessee, Kentucky, North Carolina, Virginia, and West Virginia. But the Appalachia far beneath us spans oceans. No, really. When the mountains first formed during the time of Pangaea, they covered half the world. When the land of Pangaea broke apart, it carried remains of this mountain chain across the globe; forming the mountains of the British Isles, the Scottish Highlands,

Scandinavia, and the Little Atlas mountain range of Morocco. This may explain why Scottish and Irish immigrants felt so at home here: they really just moved from one end of this mountain range to the other.

APPALACHIAN WEATHER AND SEASONS

The Appalachian Mountains influence a range of weather patterns and seasons, which the old folk counted on as signs to ensure a good harvest. Spring here is filled with a confusion of rain and sunshine. We often have what the Cherokee called "false springs"; the weather will warm up, it'll rain, and all the snow will be gone. Then come next week we might be under a couple feet of snow. The valleys of the mountains protect us from most of the hazardous weather sent our way, such as tornadoes and bad blizzards in the winter. The mountaintops take the brunt of most of that and give us a storm weaker than it might have been.

Bears who gave birth in January now lead their cubs out of their caves for the first time to forage on berries and plants to get their systems up and going. Come the first few nights of spring rain, male salamanders make their way across the forest floor to the vernal pools, where the females will soon join them. Once there, a spring orgy begins to ensure the next generation. Water from these pools is excellent in fertility work—if you're lucky enough to go at the right time.

Annually, we have what Tennessee lore names "little winters," which foreshadow the approaching end of the cold season. There'll be frequent drops in temperature that last a couple of days to a couple of weeks, followed by spring blooms of specific plants. The folks here talk about little winters just like summer and fall because they *are* seasons to us.

The first little winter occurs in early April and is called redbud winter, as this is the time that the redbud trees have stepped up on the mountain stage. Superstition says that Judas was hanged from a redbud, and another tale says if you stick a pocketknife in the tree on August 21, the tree will die.

In late April comes dogwood winter, when the dogwood trees are in bloom for a short period that ends with their petals covering lawns like snow. Any wounds acquired in dogwood winter will heal very slowly and may even scar. This is connected to the old tale that dogwood was used to make the cross on which Jesus was crucified (though it doesn't grow naturally in Israel). The tree was cursed to shrink and become twisted so it may never be used for that purpose again. The five petals of the dogwood blooms represent the five wounds Christ suffered at the crucifixion, with each petal having a point at the end. These points, along with the crown of stamens in the center, form the crown of the thorns. The representation is complete with the maroon splotch in the center, said to be the drop of Jesus's blood. Dogwood root or bark is bound to a cross with red thread and hung in the living room for protection. Between the time the dogwoods start blooming and the next new moon is the right time for farmers to plant their corn. Carry dogwood bark or root for protection from enchantment, but never bring dogwood blooms into the home or burn the bark inside on the hearth, as it's said to bring bad luck.

Next comes locust winter in early May. It's said that lightning strikes locust trees more often than others, and for this reason they're used to divine a future love interest. At this time of year, saplings are dug up from the woods and planted in the front yard of one's house—one for each potential or current lover. Each tree is named after the beloved, and the tree that thrives and grows past midsummer is the one who truly loves you. And for those who do not, their bush will die. (If more than one tree lives, the one with the thickest foliage and the sturdiest stock is the truest love.) The catch is that you cannot water the trees; they are to be nourished solely by nature. Otherwise, you will favor one over the others and mess up the divination.

Blackberry winter follows with a show of the awesome white blooms of the blackberry bush in the middle of May. An old English belief that has survived here warns that it is unlucky to eat blackberries on or after September 29, as that's when the Devil steps over the bushes with his cloven hooves. Those who do are said to die before the year ends. In Scotland, it's believed the Devil spat on the bush after landing on it from his fall from heaven. It's also said that the blackberry bush provided the thorns for Christ's crown on the cross; and many still believe the burning bush was a blackberry.

The last little winter usually occurs when the whip-poor-wills can be heard and is named as such. This one isn't as cold as the others and rarely damages plants, but it's still cold enough to keep the winter wear out a bit longer. Some folks call it the ghost winter or phantom winter, as the outward signs of winter have vanished. While these winters are a part of our folklore and ecosystem, they are likely to disappear altogether as climate change worsens.

During these winters, a symphony of flowers arrives to the Appalachian landscape, blooming and disappearing over and over. Folks are off to Easter dinners, getting into spring cleaning in the attics and closets. That brisk breeze that flows through the open windows and doors while Mama cleans are the best after a cold winter. Spring tonics are drunk to get one's system back on track for the warm months, and the debris of fall and winter are cleared from the gardens. Now the mountains are fully awake with life: deer stalking behind the brush, turkey vultures looking for a field feast, and foxes roaming sometimes where foxes ought not to roam.

High summer comes with abundance of corn, tobacco, and squash. Folks are off to the lakes and rivers to cool off, and the mountains are lush with greenery. In high summer, I would be in the creeks catching tadpoles and minnows or up the mountain sitting and watching the deer graze. However, this fun was tempered by the superstitions of my mother and grandmother, especially during the dog days, which runs from July 3 to August 11. Folks believed dogs caught rabies more at this time than any other; snakes were meaner; and misfortune was more apt to be found. At this time the star Sirius moves with the sun, bringing misfortune as it goes from horizon to horizon. The tiniest cut could quickly become a dangerous infection, and you were more likely to drown. Late summer crops, like tomatoes and okra, had to be harvested before the animals or blight got them.

After the summer solstice passes and the fireflies' light shows are done, nature begins to hush. Just before the autumn equinox the corn is gathered and the tobacco is speared on the stakes. Then there's the final weeding of the garden and the dirt is turned over with debris of the garden to fertilize the soil.

This was the time that livestock was slaughtered to store up on food and to cut down the mouths that need fed on winter mornings. The mountains become ablaze with life's last moments as animals forage and store away food for the winter. With the bear cubs long grown and a generation of salamanders passed, Mother Appalachia begins shedding her garments accompanied by rainstorms, sleeping crickets, and a show of falling leaves.

Mother Mountain takes her leave for sleep and we are left chilled. The leaves have long been brown and will now see a time of freezing and melting before the earth accepts them back in decomposition. Most animals are hibernating, yet some brave the mountain winter. A lone deer, hog, coyote, or turkey will still rummage through the bones of the forest, and Mother Mountain hides her face behind low skies. The wind is the only sound on the land. The temperature drops sometimes below zero, branches are covered with ice, and the crows and hawks are the only citizens of the sky, foraging for those not strong enough for the cold. Then the robin heralds the first signs of spring in

February, bringing with her the fire of summer painted on her chest, and the whole cycle begins again.

APPALACHIAN TERRAIN

The terrain of these mountains is ever changing due in part to our weather patterns. In some parts, the forest floor is covered in old pine needles, while in other places there are grassy patches. Rocky cliffs, steep riverbanks, and mossy hills are in the mix as well. The trees are spaced by their choosing, limbs knotting under nature's hand, and the green lake waters stir only by the breeze and an occasional bass or trout.

The old folk traversed these hills in nothing more than their britches and boots. But some of these mountains are so steep you must hold on to younger trees as you climb and pray the wood is sturdy enough to hold your weight should you slip. I often climbed Big Ridge Mountain when I was little. It was just like this, until it levels out and the trees open up to show the valleys below, with the occasional free-ranging cow grazing in the distance.

The rivers are littered with boulders older than the dirt on the banks. As the water rushes past, it splashes these boulders and stones, encouraging the growth of moss and grass. The eddies created by the boulders make safe places for the minnows to rest. If you hold your feet still enough in the creeks, they'll come up and start nibbling the dead skin off.

Then there are the fields. The original colonizers described Appalachia as the endless forest. The only fields here prior to settling were made by the Cherokee, who cleared trees to make room for their gardens and homes. But even the Cherokee say there are some they didn't create, like the grassy balds near Roan Mountain. Said to be the largest balds in the world, they are described as being the footprints of the Devil as he walked over the Blue Ridge. Right around dawn, the deer and turkeys come out to graze, and groundhogs are also a common sight.

We have natural springs and pools that seem to come from another world. The people of Appalachia have always had a good relationship with water, and both the Cherokee and the Baptists baptize their children in the river. Many people spend their summers at the lakes and springs. During this heat the animals' priority becomes water to drink, so you'll sometimes see deer mosey down to the water too, standing just a few yards away.

APPALACHIAN HISTORY

Now nature and places ain't all that's in these hills. We also have a rich history, deeply woven into the birthing walls of America. I'm only speaking of the history in East Tennessee and surrounding areas here. To include the history of all of Appalachia would take more time than either of us have got.

By the late seventeenth century, when English immigrants arrived in East Tennessee, the Cherokee had become the region's dominant tribe and had established small towns scattered about the mountains and valleys. The Cherokee are an Iroquoian-speaking tribe thought to have originated in the Great Lakes region. However, another theory is that the Iroquois migrated north to their present place while the Cherokee stayed in this proposed "origin place."

There's a Cherokee myth recorded in the eighteenth century that says when the Cherokee first arrived here they found "moon-eyed" people living in the mountains. They were called moon-eyed because they couldn't see well during the day. They had white skin, blonde hair, and gray eyes. They are said to have been the creators of the pre-Columbian ruins found scattered in the hills. The Cherokee battled the "moon-eyed" people, sending them westward after they were defeated.

Cherokee society is traditionally matriarchal—a person's lineage is traced through their mother—and women were held in high regard. This respect for the elderly woman remains in Appalachia. Each Cherokee woman belonged to a family clan, and no one could mate with someone of their same clan. When a man wanted marriage, he would have to build a woman a house. If she wanted a divorce, she would gather his things while he was out hunting and set them on the porch. She got to keep everything else, including the house and children. When this happened, the mother's uncles and brothers would fulfill the father's duties in teaching the sons how to hunt, pray, and fight. This same kind of structure is in place in most Appalachian families.

When immigrants began showing up in the mountains in the late seventeenth century, there was hostility between them and the natives. The Cherokee freely gave land to the settlers, but they wanted more. And they kept taking it and killing for it. Treaty after treaty was broken. Most white folks thought the Indian a barbaric animal. Others, however, were kind to the Cherokee and gladly shared the mountains.

In 1830 the Indian Removal Act was enacted, and in 1838 the Cherokee nation was forced west. This was the infamous Trail of Tears. The stories about it are still told at the International Storytelling Center in Jonesborough and at Sycamore Shoals State Park in Elizabethton. About seventeen thousand Cherokee were forcibly removed; between two and six thousand died along the way. Most of them were moved west of the Mississippi River, but some stayed behind and hid in the groves of the mountains.

The Indian wars, the genocide, and the removal all contributed to the loss of wisdom from the natives—their stories, annual traditions, crafts, and herbal knowledge. Eventually, the Cherokee who stayed bought back their own land. Today, the Eastern Band of Cherokee Indians is the only tribe in America that doesn't live on a reservation. Sadly, their territory, the Qualla Boundary, has become a tourist spot for white folks, and the Cherokee wear headdresses to "look the part." Historically, Cherokee never wore such things. The men shaved their whole head, save for one braid in the back usually adorned with a feather. Thankfully, not all of the Cherokee stories were lost. It's the stories that carry the spirit of a people, regardless of traditions or techniques lost and forgotten. If the stories survive, so do the people. The Cherokee have attained a population count, West and East, of five hundred thousand registered people, and many are working to keep their stories and language alive. However, only about three thousand speak their native language, Tsalagi, fluently.

APPALACHIAN FOLK MAGIC

Appalachian folk magic came about because it gave these people a sense that things were going to be alright even in the poor circumstances most found themselves in. It let them get a handle on things, one way or another. And it works. While you won't get rich quick, you can use it to better the circumstances the world sets against you, even if you're still piss-poor afterward. With it, you can foresee the cards you're about to be dealt and change the tables somewhat in your favor.

Appalachian conjure was kept secret mostly from those with a suspicion and mistrust for it—usually the well-off church folk who sat on their own pedestal every Sunday morning. Anything "primitive" or deemed "against the good book" was of the Devil himself. Mamaw scrunched her nose at those people. You can go to every church in Unicoi, Carter, and Washington counties, but that ain't making you right with the Lord. When the well-off folks are in trouble, they'll need someone and won't be able to get the "special" help they need.

American folk magic is a melting pot of practices stemming from Irish, Scottish, German, Italian, and other European sources as well as African and Native American sources. For example, the uses of different waters like rainwater and ocean water originates mostly from the

British Isles. The use of dirts and dusts comes from the Native Americans and the African slaves brought to this land. The act of placing bowls and pans under the bed for works or spells comes from Jewish folklore; the practice of throwing spells and remnants behind oneself into a stream comes from European traditions; and the use of grave dirt comes from African and European traditions.

It can be difficult to discern where methods and practices originally came from, especially with generations of change and adaptation. Some things are added or taken away based on location, timing, and need. That's why you will always find a handful of spell recipes for the same purpose but with varying ingredients or tools. For example, hotfoot powder, which is used to make folks leave you alone or even leave town, sometimes consists of hot peppers, spices, and sulfur. But those things aren't found often here in the mountains, so most people mix black pepper and salt instead, as they are cheap and readily available. I've also heard of adding spiders, bugs, and other things to scare or chase folks away. We don't call it "hotfoot" in the mountains, either: to us it's "uprooting" people to make them leave and never return.

Although some prefer to stick to tradition, these roots grow and change. We can honor and trust in the strength and support they gave through the racism, genocide, and persecution our old folks suffered. Through all the troubles, they preserved the knowledge and practices that helped make everything bearable and gave our ancestors an upper hand against the trials that held them.

These hills have been soaked in blood, covered with bones, and have resounded with cries of war and birth over and over. They've witnessed life and death occur more times than our minds can comprehend. Their soil has been stained by the blood of soldiers and slaves alike. These same struggles have given rise to our culture today in the form of tradition, folk songs and art, and good cooking.

Our weather and seasons and landscape shaped the way we farm and plant, the foods we hunt and grow, and the remedies we created for ourselves when the mountains locked us in. But it wasn't just with us that the mountains did this. They've been shaping the culture, practices, and magic of people as long as they've been inhabited, even long before the Cherokee put down roots here. Very likely, the land of your folks did the same to your family and community.

History here is weaved into the spider's web. The river runs warm with the paranormal, and witchcraft whispers on foggy autumn mornings just before the church bells start ringing. Let's now turn to the superstitions and tales of these hills: those bedtime stories that may have root in dream or history, echoes of haints in the graveyard, and chills when an unseen guest is knocking at the door. Superstition is the fuel behind folk magic. Of course, we don't think it to be primitive or backward; it's what the old folks always did and said, so we do the same because they got along alright with it. Personally, I can validate that most of these tales are true. Superstition finds its spot nestled around the needs of humanity, whether it be food, weather, hunting, childbearing, or labor. It guides us from accidentally bringing ill onto ourselves and offers protection from the same from others. It is there, in the pit of those needs, that mountain witchcraft and healing is born, cultivated, and preserved across generations.

2

DOWN DEVIL'S RUN
Stories and Superstitions

The stories and superstitions that run through these hills are one place you can find witchcraft and conjure, whether it's in the methods of precaution prescribed against bad luck or tidbits of how to heal a disease. There are stories of odd creatures in the wild, women keening for their lost loves, and the Devil himself laughing over the river. We'll begin with the latter.

Located outside of Erwin, Tennessee, overlooking the Nolichucky River, the Devil's Looking Glass is a haunted cliff of rock standing hundreds of feet tall and covered with the fingerprints of death. There are countless tales of this mountain cliff and the waters that churn below, but I'll recount only a couple here. The first is of a Cherokee woman who threw herself off the cliff. The story goes that she and her lover were very close, and he was taken into battle to fight for his people. He didn't return. The woman's grief overtook her, and she climbed to the top of the cliff and jumped, calling for her lost love as she fell. Many people have seen her wading in the waters below, keening for her mate. Others say that early in the morning, you can hear her singing for her lover to return to her, a song that turns to crying and wailing as the day grows old.

Other stories of the cliff tell of banshee cries in the area. It's said that a man and his pregnant wife lived in a cabin along the river, two miles away from the nearest neighbor. One night the man heard a sound coming from down the river and mistook it to be the cries of a bobcat. The old man, expecting to get a new pelt, wandered down the riverbank, following the sound. As he wandered, he noticed that the sound didn't seem to be getting any closer. And at one point, the sound seemed to be coming from the other direction. After hours of searching, he gave up and started back to his cabin. When he arrived, he found his wife in labor. Hours later, both his wife and the baby died.

I have personal experience with this. My grandparents lived up on a hill near a wooded area that led to a graveyard. One day, while playing in the forest, I heard a cry. It was odd because it sounded like a cat but also a woman's scream. It didn't happen in the usual pattern ascribed to an animal in heat; instead, it sounded like an alarm. Within the week, my grandfather died of his seventh heart attack.

Now, the banshee didn't kill my grandfather, and it didn't kill the woman and her baby in the other story, either. On the contrary, banshees are considered a type of "little folk" that came over with European immigrants, and they are one of the few spirits of who care for humans. They just come to warn of death and mourn the person's passing, and it's thought they are drawn to anyone with strong Irish blood. Irish stories describe the banshee as a woman who stays near water to wash her grave-stained robes. They say she has bloodshot eyes from crying for the dead. Banshees were also said to have a comb stuck in their hair, so it's always been a bad omen to find a discarded comb on the ground.

Another old tale of the Devil's Looking Glass says that a witch named Ol' Miz Wilson lived in a cabin near the rocky bottom of the cliffs, and would call up the restless dead from the river and entertain them with charms and spells. Her parties ended at sunrise, at which time the spirits returned to the rocks and beds. After her death, it was said that every Halloween at midnight, the rocks in the cliff grow eyes: the eyes of the spirits are looking for something to entertain them again.

The creepiest tale I was told growing up was, if you stood on the banks before the Devil's Looking Glass on a real foggy morning, you could chance to see the Devil himself shaving in the mirror and laughing at you. This isn't the only association the Devil has with the Nolichucky River. There are tales of a "lone rider" who rides up and down the banks on moonless nights. It's said you'll hear the hoofbeats get closer and closer until they're right up on you, at which point you'll hear them go off in the other direction and die down without ever seeing a living soul. No one could ever get a clear view of who the rider was that was scaring folk—only an occasional blurred shadow on the bank that passed by fast as ever.

A couple decades ago, a few men took it upon themselves to get to the bottom of who this rider was. They camped on the bank overnight, waiting for the rider to show. One person stayed up to keep watch. Around 3:00 a.m., the watchman began to hear hoofbeats down the river. He woke the others up and they scrambled around, tying a rope to a tree at the water's edge and holding the other end some ten yards back. Their plan was to pull on the rope to trip the horse and throw the rider off right when they passed.

The hoofbeats got closer and closer; the men readied themselves. A shadowy blur passed by and with a force it pulled on the rope, yanking the men forward on their faces. The hoofbeats continued in the other direction, their pattern and beat unhindered by the rope or the men's efforts. The men were confused. One suggested it couldn't be a ghost because it pulled on the rope. Then they saw hoofprints in the mud, and validated it wasn't a ghost because ghosts don't leave footprints in the mud.

However, upon further investigation they found the hoofprints weren't U-shaped like a horse's. They were cloven, like a goat. it was at that point the men ran back home yelling, "it was the Devil himself!" No one dared look for the identity of the rider again. For this story, the river was named Devil's Run. Stories have warned since not to be caught out on the banks at night alone or else the Devil may challenge you to a race for your soul. What do you reckon your chances are of winning?

There are countless accounts of unexplained deaths and missing victims at the Nolichucky River. The water unexpectedly rises and the current's strength intensifies without warning. It happens so often, there've been plenty of times we've found dead animals on the shores, taken down and drowned in an instant. Whether it's lovers camping on the banks or deer stopping for a nighttime drink, the river has consumed many lives. Because of its dangerous nature, the Cherokee called the river Black Waters.

There have been accounts of transparent fishermen standing on the shore holding fishing rods, while others tell of children playing in the waters only to disappear behind their own splashing. Common sense tells folks to avoid this area altogether at night or without company. While it's still a great spot for fishing and kayaking, many still get an eerie feeling while gazing at the rapid currents cutting their way between the mountains.

We also have our share of ghosts. Ghost stories have been a major portion of storytelling in these hills, and we hear them from a young age. While mostly reserved for camping trips and time spent waiting for Halloween night, most of these stories are passed down in the family and are told whenever the children ask. My family went every year to the Cherokee festival at Sycamore Shoals, so I also grew up on the old Cherokee tales of bears and blue-corn beads, stories of the witch Selu and her sons, Kanati the Lucky Hunter, as well as tales of the saints and haints in the hills. Before my generation, everyone listened to the stories of the elders, and these stories were stored in their bones and teeth, so they could be recounted and told again in other times and places. Thankfully, I was one of those who listened.

Of course, not all haints and creatures are benign, and the old folks knew that. For this reason, there are superstitions, sayings, and charms to teach and protect people from hauntings and evil spirits. For instance, tying a red piece of yarn to your right upper arm or setting knives up in the windows will do just that. And sewing a piece of red ribbon into the inner lining of your shoe heel will protect you from ghosts making you sick.

Going through these stories, one can see the close relationship we often build with these spirits, loving them like family unless they cause harm. For those spirits that were troublesome, preachers were often asked to come and clear the home. My grandfather did so frequently, among his other gifts of blood stopping and wart charming. One saying my family always uses to get rid of a haint or troublesome spirit is to ask it, "What in the name of the Lord do you want?" and it should stop.

By now you're probably wondering how these stories have any connection to folk magic. The tales show the mind-set that mountain folk have had for centuries in these hills, mirroring that of their ancestors in the Old World. This same mind-set was held by the native peoples.

Back in the day, people would come home from church on Sunday and be just fine with talking to the dead that roamed their land. These stories are woven on battlefields, embroidered by the pulpit and choir, and hung on the clothesline in the holler, in the yard of the lonesome sinner. Each tale adds to the culture and community beliefs of the people of Appalachia. These tales are both the mother and child of superstition at its greatest. They teach us to be kind and careful, but stern and strong. They teach us to mind our own most of the time, and what will happen should we act otherwise. When was the last time an old tale talked about someone who wasn't snooping around places? Following are some of the superstitions and beliefs I was raised on in East Tennessee.

SUPERSTITIONS AND CHARMS

Stories and superstitions often intersect, like a complex dream catcher. There's very little distinction between the two, based on their particular origin. Here I will share some of the good ol' superstitions and tricks of these hills.

Witches

Here is the perfect place to fill you in about what mountain folks think of witches and how they differ from the doctors and healers. Witches were thought to have made pacts with the Devil, read the Bible backward, and consulted with demons to gain their conjuring knowledge. This belief stems from Europe, primarily, where these same beliefs are rampant throughout records of the Inquisition.

Witches were said to go through initiations into black magic, whether it was shooting a silver bullet at the Bible while cursing Jehovah or waiting in the family cemetery for the Devil to arrive and have intercourse with him. While most accounts of true witchcraft follow no such belief, it is apparent that the reputation of a conjure person was primarily based on the attitude of the community. The yarb doctor was seen as a circumstance-born healer, gifted by God; and although they could be found mixing up some revenge for a client's enemy, they were still labeled "good," as the community believed their powers to be a gift of the Most High.

The witch, on the other hand, was susceptible to a much harsher judgment from society. It was believed that the outcast, crazy woman up the holler was mixing up poisons, dancing with the Devil, and tossing curses from her perch. There are stories of witches charming cats and collecting them in bags, cursing cattle, and blasting crops. Those that were documented in these tales were the yarb doctors. But of course that was fine, because the community thought well of them; the rest were often unverified tales. The lines between the witch and yarb doctor are blurred at best and nonexistent at times, save for the reputation given them by the community.

There are many stories that have made their way over from the Green Isle, telling of folks getting lost and taken in by the wee ones, and also acquiring knowledge and gifts from the little folk. Others are simply "marked by God." This term is used to denote those who are born in certain circumstances such as having a caul over the eyes; being a seventh son or daughter; being born a surviving or "left" twin; being born feetfirst; or being born through C-section or blue. I am a member of the latter, having been born with fluid in my lungs because I took my first breath in the womb. Nana once said that's why I've always been good with animals and know when something's wrong with folks, cause I "know what's inside 'em," or how things are. This is referred to as the gift or sight and is spoken of, softly, by the families who still recognize its presence. Having these "marks" is said to happen to those that will walk the banks between this world and the next. This "gift" isn't a psychic ability, however. We aren't born with it naturally or genetically. It is something given exclusively by God and the spirits. Most of these folks have experiences of seeing spirits from a young age. I have not had the experience of seeing fully materialized spirits, per se, but I do hear and feel them, with the occasional waist-to-head view of them, but I can't figure any hard details.

Until recently, these situations at birth were considered medically dangerous and filled mothers with worry when the doctor informed her of her child's "condition." Nowadays, these things aren't paid much attention and the information is not usually given to the mother. As a result, many would-be healers never know of their gift or why they see or hear things.

There are tales of power doctors getting their knowledge from an encounter with the little folk or simply being blessed from birth. Regardless of the tales, it has been the reputation of the worker in the community that speaks of their power's origin and their moral compass. My mother says my knack for remembering so much of this is due to me walking around under a black bull when I was little. Said it nearly gave her a heart attack, but I was a curious child. Especially when I wasn't being watched.

Protection

The old-timers have always been superstitious when it comes to ghosts, lightning, death, witches, and curses. Basically anything that could threaten their livelihood. While some of the following formulas leave no explanation for their reasoning, they are still practiced today because, as I was always told, "It's just what the old folks did." These remedies and charms are tradition, and you aren't supposed to question it. No one does. With no rhyme or reason, these tricks and charms have continued in these hills, containing the fragments of their parent cultures and the fixing-thoughts of the mountaineers. And they work—so why question them?

The most important people in the household who warranted protection from haints and the evil eye were children. Children are most susceptible to these threats in their earliest months, and it is customary to christen and baptize babies as soon as possible. Yarrow is hung at the head of the crib and an iron nail can be driven into the post of the crib to protect the child from being taunted or taken by the little folk. If the child got sick, some folks would bring the child to the preacher or some other type of healer. My mother, a seventh daughter blessed with the power to heal, had to only rub our bellies a certain way and by the next sunrise we were fine. The previous symptoms were commonly thought of among the Old Irish as signs that a changeling, a double, sat in the crib while the real babe was lost somewhere in faery land.

Belief in changelings didn't fully make their way to Appalachia, but there are some rituals that were done to see if the babe had indeed been stolen away: one was to carry the child around a balefire while saying the Lord's Prayer. The only sign that it is human will be if the child sneezes.

Chamomile-infused milk was also fed to the infant nightly for the first six months of their life to protect them from evil and to preserve their life until dawn. When a child died from sudden infant death syndrome (SIDS), it was believed that it was the work of the Devil or a mischievous spirit, so people naturally took up arms with measures to prevent it from happening again. However, although children are considered the most vulnerable, the elders saw power in their innocence and their purity from true sin. Because of this, they prized things made by children as powerful trinkets of protection, an American legacy that can be seen in the common child-gifts for protection in movies and literature. One such superstition calls for a seven-year-old girl to spin thread on Good Friday, Sunday, or Christmas Day (it varies based on location and family tradition). This thread was then sewn into the hem of britches and shirts to guard one from disease, evil spirits, and curses.

After the children and elders, your own self is next in line. There are a number of things one can do for protection: carry an iron nail in the left pocket to protect yourself from the activities of the little folk or wrap a horseshoe in aluminum foil and hang it over the door. A horseshoe wrapped in red cloth and hung upside down for Wednesday, Thursday, and Friday will help get rid of haints. I'll discuss these rites in more detail in chapter 6.

As we know, the weather of Appalachia can be unpredictable in both season and severity, and lightning can be particularly threatening. Folks would walk around the home tapping two stones together to create a barrier that lightning couldn't penetrate. This was done with one black stone and one white stone. The Cherokee believed that wood from a tree that has been struck by lightning will protect from the same and give the person who wears it power. Geranium petals are also said to protect from lightning (as well as dog bites).

When restless or troublesome spirits come to haunt the household, the potato charm is utilized. One acquires a whole, unwashed potato and a small object that belonged to the deceased. The potato is cut in half and each side is hollowed out, made large enough for the item to fit snugly inside. The halves are then reunited, bound with red yarn, and pinned shut with nails. The charm is then taken to the grave of the spirit, where it is left. The spirit will then be bound to the cemetery until they fully cross over.

Other practices include hanging bunches of basil over the windows and doors to keep unwanted spirits out, hanging lavender to protect from misfortune, and placing a dried corncob beneath the doorway to attract good fortune and keep disease away. In order for this to work, though, the corncob must always remain dry, or it will mold and rot away the luck.

To protect yourself from being "witched" or "hoodooed," tie up a lock of your hair, a toenail clipping, and a stick from the "sunny" or eastern side of an oak with red string, while invoking the name of the Father, the Son, and the Holy Spirit. It's said you can't be cursed or worked on as long as you have this charm on your person. However, should you ever lose the charm, the person who finds it can use it to curse you.

The lock of hair and the nail paring shows the importance of the head and feet, which are the most powerful ways a witch can lay roots on someone, by either dusting one's head while asleep or rooting on your footprints. (We'll go over the importance of the head and feet more in chapter 6.) The hair and nails also act as a decoy, luring any tricks to it first, because curses take the shortest route to the target (in this case, the charm). The oak has a long history of protection and strength. As these are bound with the red string, symbolic of blood, one is bound outside of the grasp of curses and enchantments.

To remove curses or tricks, one carries a piece of coal in the right pocket or shoe. Once the coal has diminished to dust and crumbs, the curse has been removed. The crumbs are then disposed of at a cross-roads or beneath a willow tree that stands next to a stream. Return a different way than you came, and cross the stream as well. The reason being the crossroads will contain the curse in a kind of "prison"; before real grave markers, the willow tree stood as a marker of graves in Appalachia for a long period. Today, they are places to "put things to rest," and you should cross the stream to deter anything from lingering or following you.

Good Luck

Life in Appalachia was hard enough without the extra misfortune that fate dealt. Closely following the concept of protection, there are tricks and wits to bring good luck and keep misfortune away. My grand-mothers always hung horseshoes pointing upward to keep the luck from running out.

Another tradition was always keeping a jar of money by the door to keep the money coming in. The jar was filled with money that one found on the sidewalk or elsewhere, and it was collected in anything, from an empty peanut butter jar to an old crock pot. Cornmeal was always sprinkled at the bottom to make a soft "dirt" for the money and to keep it off the hard bottom so likewise the family would be kept off hard times. And let me tell you, no matter how hard life was, we were always given or found some money and not a day went by that we didn't have some type of food to eat as long as that jar sat by the door. When you find money, you should pick up the coin or dollar and place it in your left pocket until it can be added to the jar. Money from the jar can be spent, but it should never be totally emptied and should always hold seven or more of one type of currency (for example, seven dimes, seven pennies, or seven one-dollar bills).

You of course know that four-leaf clovers and ladybugs are lucky, and it's the same here in Appalachia. However, a four-leaf clover has to be found when you *aren't* looking for it, and no one else can ever see the clover or it will lose its power. To keep a found four-leaf clover secret, folks would tuck it away in their Bible along with their own picture under the clover, or else they'd put it in their Bible cover. Some folks would even sew clovers in the rim of hats or in the inner lining of their shoes.

Good luck also comes if you find a four-holed button or a heads-up penny and put it in your right shoe. A spider found nesting in the kitchen is another sign of luck and abundance and would never be disturbed. The family would never go hungry as long as it made camp. Seeing the new moon for the first time each month over your left shoulder is also considered good luck, but not if you see it through the trees.

Old folks also weren't afraid of using animal parts and leftovers for remedies and charms. Whether they cooked worms by the fire to make an oil for arthritis or rubbed rabbit brains on the gums for toothache, they weren't the least bit squeamish. Therefore, many animal parts and bones are used for good luck and gambling. The most famous is the bone of a black cat.

Black cats are notoriously thought to be bad luck. Old formulas called for using the bones of a black cat. The skeleton was taken to a creek where the water flows to the south and the bones were dropped into the water. One bone would float and go upstream; it's that one bone that will be lucky. Other variations call for it to be done in the woods or simply in the home; or the "creek" is replaced with a pot of milk, into which the hot bones are dropped and either the first one to come to the surface or whine like a cat was the lucky bone.

These bone-washing formulas, as I call them, derive from Europe, and over time they have been adapted to be more humane. More recent tales specify using the bones of a naturally deceased black cat.

The formulas and charms I use were recommended by the old-timers in these mountains. For example, a bone from the right paw of an opossum is carried for luck and success, which works just as well. Other good luck charms are deer horn points worn around the neck, which also protect from the evil eye, or a muskrat or rabbit's foot carried on the person.

Bad Luck

Bad luck was something mountain folk just couldn't afford. If the crops began to rot or someone had an accident and couldn't get care, it could decimate their daily lives. So, they listened close to Granny's "tall tales," lest fate be tempted. Here are a few things to be wary of:

- It is bad luck to open an umbrella inside the house, to come in a door you didn't go out from, and to spill salt or oil.

- Don't burn sassafras or pinewood in the home.

- Burning cedar or dogwood inside is also said to bring bad luck.

- Likewise, dogwood blooms shouldn't ever be brought into the house, because it's said that's the wood Jesus hung from at Calvary.

- When a new candle is brought into the house, the wick must be lit and immediately snuffed to keep bad luck out.

- Women weren't allowed at the coal mines, as most people believed they would bring bad luck to the mine.

- When a fish is caught, the fish should be thanked or bad luck will befall the home and the cabinets will be bare within the season.

- To point at a graveyard, especially one with a new grave in it, will invite sickness and death.

It is in these superstitions that the old folks sometimes went to the extremes. Bad stuff was terrifying for them and could literally end their lives as they knew it. They went to the extreme even in medicine, ingesting turpentine or kerosene, for example. I can say that a hundred more times, but you won't know the truth of it unless you're from here. Extreme measures included wearing powdered gizzards or manure in the shoes to keep off conjuring, carrying a rag with dried blood from a bull's ankle for health and vigor, or drinking sheep nanny tea for measles, which was made from sheep manure.

HEALING

Modern medical services weren't widely available in Appalachia for quite some time, so folks relied on old charms and remedies for their ailments, just as their immigrant ancestors had done. Warts were fairly common and irritating due to poor hygiene of the time. My grandfather could wipe a wart off with a rag and a prayer or buy it from you.

Sadly, Papaw passed on before I could learn about this particular method for removing warts, but my mother taught me one that's a bit more involved but works just as well. Quartzite, known here as mountain quartz, is abundant in the fields and streams. The charm uses these white stones picked from a creek that flows south or west. You take up the same number of stones as warts that need to be removed. The stones are picked from the creek, but one must go with the river's flow to get them. So, you take your hand and follow the current in the same direction as you lower your hand down in the water to snatch up the stone, taking care to not disturb the flow of water as you drop your hand down to the creek bed or as you come back up with the stone. It's believed that if the current is disturbed, it annoys the spirits. Each stone is then touched to a wart three times and placed in a small pouch and then hung on a cow's horns or a fence post in a field, or left at the crossroads to wait for the next person who will open the bag of warts and get them.

My grandfather had a gift for stopping the flow of blood. Not many people can do this successfully or even as great as he could, in my opinion. Sometimes, he would indirectly stop a woman's flow. There are a couple methods I've heard of. One requires a rag that is dampened with holy water and left out overnight on Christmas Eve. This rag is used throughout the year to stop wounds from bleeding, much like an Irish brat being left out to be blessed by the Goddess Brigit on February 1.

The other method for stopping bleeding entails passing the left hand clockwise over the wound while reciting the following words, quiet enough so the patient cannot hear:

> *Jesus was born in Bethlehem,*
> *Baptized in the Jordon River.*
> *When the water was wild in the woods,*
> *God spoke and the water stood,*
> *And so shall thy blood.*
> *In the name of the Father, the Son, and the Holy Spirit.*
> *Amen.*

Papaw told my mom he couldn't cross running water for twenty-four hours after performing this rite. To cross it would undo the charm and the blood would flow again. Another practice he did was he'd give the person a red string to tie around their neck or on their left wrist to stop the blood. It was believed the blood would be stopped by the knot in the yarn.

Water is another form of powerful medicine. Water collected at daybreak on Easter Morning, Good Friday, or Ash Wednesday is said to be a cure for multiple illnesses. Rainwater from the gutters is applied to rashes and the "water" (urine) collected from a cow is tossed onto someone's feet to change their luck around. The least known but most powerful of waters would be stump water. The old folks often called it spunk water because it sometimes has an odd smell; this is probably dependent on the tree it is collected from.

Water found in the grooves of boulders was given the same respect, as it had also never touched the soil. Likewise, in Ireland we find the noted healing belief in well water whose surface had never been touched or "broken" by man. (This will be covered more in chapter 10.)

Ocean water is known to help heal anything from deep wounds to rheumatoid arthritis. My grandmother had knee surgery and for months afterward was plagued by painful knees. Some cousins were vacationing at the beach, and she called them up and told them to fill a big jar with some ocean water. They brought back a five-gallon pickle jar of seawater, big enough that my grandmother put both her legs in and soaked them to relieve the pain. She did that for a week, and her knees have never bothered her as bad since.

Besides charms and magical waters, the people of Appalachia have relied on home remedies and herbal medicines for healing. For croup, we drink the juices of a baked onion. For rashes, we mash plantain into a paste and apply it generously. We had the common sense that herbs may not always work, so our remedies often included man's medicine or chemicals. Whether turpentine, cod liver oil, or lard, we tried different things and kept the ones that worked. When I was little, I personally despised the hot toddy my grandmother would make and give to us had she heard a pitch when we coughed. I now cherish it as one of my best cures!

For a common cold, Mama always said to get two cloves of garlic and cut them in half. Take a half from each and tie them to the person's feet, right on their soles. Within about an hour, their breath would smell like garlic, at which point Mama would take the tied cloves and chuck them out the back door. The other two halves were then replaced and the same process was repeated. After the second round of cloves had been thrown out, they'd soak their feet in warm saltwater to "pull the cold out."

MARKING AND MIRRORING

I grew up hearing about children being marked by their mothers in the womb by things the mother did. I'm one example. When my mother was three months pregnant with me, she was thrown out of a moving truck going 75 miles per hour. Thankfully, we were both okay, but I was born with a birthmark on my back in the shape of a pickup truck. The belief is that if the mother is frightened by something, her baby could be marked with a birthmark the shape of what frightened her, or have a physical resemblance to the something or someone. On the other hand, the babe could be marked by someone the mother loved dearly. My godson, whose mother is my best friend, has a dimple on his upper cheek just like mine that shows when he smiles.

This also applies anytime the mother goes against a taboo, such as walking over a grave or going to a funeral. A baby born to a woman who does this will be born pale and ghostly, or with a deformity. Or if a pregnant woman has a major craving for something that can't be fully satisfied, her baby will be born with some kind of physical evidence of it. One of my cousins craved strawberries all the time while she was pregnant, and her son was born with a birthmark on his ankle shaped like a strawberry. There's no logic behind these sayings, but I've seen them be fulfilled enough times to believe it.

The behavior of the mother could also mark the baby. If she is whiny while pregnant, she will have a whiny kid. If she made fun of a disabled person, her child will be born with the same disability. The old folks didn't always render to these foreign powers. They developed their own formulas for having the child be a certain way. The marking or mirroring charms they developed mostly surround the care for a child after it is born, but not always.

The first cup of water a mother should carry after birth should be a thimble full of water. She's to carry it from the driveway up to the house and to the child without spilling a drop. This keeps the child from drooling a lot through infancy. She also shouldn't cross over running water until the child is one month old. Otherwise it's said to bring illness on both of them. The latter isn't very reasonable in today's age with concrete roads. We never know when we're traveling over a natural creek anymore.

BIRTH, LABOR, CHILDCARE

Besides those about the condition of the mother affecting her baby, there are a plethora of superstitions around divining if one is pregnant, and the birthing process. One my mother has always followed is placing an egg in a glass to determine if a woman is pregnant. First, the egg is rubbed over the woman's belly in a cross formation. The woman then blows on the egg and drops it into a clear glass of water. If the egg sinks, the woman is with child. If it floats, she is not.

This practice was often paired with a way to predict the sex of the child. A gold wedding ring was suspended from three hairs taken from the crown of the expectant mother's head. She is to lie down "as Christ was laid," Nana says, meaning her head should be pointing west. The ring is dangled over her navel and Psalm 23 is recited:

> *A Psalm of David.*
> *The LORD is my shepherd;*
> *I shall not want.*
> *He maketh me to lie down in green pastures;*
> *He leadeth me beside the still waters.*
> *He restoreth my soul;*
> *He leadeth me in the paths of righteousness for his name's sake.*
> *Yea, though I walk through the valley of the shadow of death,*
> *I will fear no evil:*
> *for thou art with me;*
> *Thy rod and thy staff they comfort me.*
> *Thou preparest a table before me*
> *in the presence of mine enemies.*
> *Thou anointest my head with oil;*
> *my cup runneth over.*
> *Surely goodness and mercy shall follow me*
> *all the days of my life,*
> *and I will dwell in the house of the LORD*
> *for ever.*

If the ring rotates in circles over her belly, it is a girl. If it swings back and forth, it is a boy.

If a woman wishes to be free from her pregnancy symptoms, especially morning sickness, all she's got to do is crawl over her lover to get out of bed in the morning. This will pass the symptoms on to him. I've seen this work multiple times. Not for the men, necessarily, but it still worked.

About 80 percent of the charms surrounding women have to do with the birthing process. This was old Appalachia, where a woman's role was to bear children. That role was very dangerous in that time. As with all things, the mountaineer took up faith and charm and used them together for aid.

To ease birthing pains, a Bible opened to the book of Matthew is placed on the woman's chest or stomach. The location depends on the necessity. If the child is in danger, the stomach; if the mother, the chest. A knife, arrowhead, or axe is also placed beneath the bed to cut the pains in pieces and render them harmless. In today's hospitals, these aren't acceptable, so make a "tea" with these boiled in water for the mother to drink.

In the case of possible hemorrhage during labor, chicken feathers were burned under the bed. A bundle of six feathers should be gathered by the father or another man of the house. If not the father, I've heard, it should be done by a graying man. It was best if the feathers were plucked straight from the chicken, but this wasn't a requirement at the time.

Birth came with sadness sometimes. Stillbirths were common in the hills. In the case of a stillborn child, the mother needed a way to dry her milk without that physical pain being added to her grief. A charm was devised for just that: camphor on a cotton wad was placed in the child's grave to dry up the mother's milk. If a woman continued to have stillborn children, Nana always said she should name the next boy Adam. He'll live and she won't have another stillborn. Typically, a child wasn't called by their birth name for much of their childhood, to keep them safe from the evil eye and haints. For most of my childhood, my family called me Bubba.

Childcare was a whole other story. Many times, charms were devised to aid the child's health, but also to ease the labor of the parents. A stuttering child was believed to be cured by drinking water from a church bell or baptism pool.

The teething phase can be hard for mother and child, but especially for a woman of old Appalachia with likely more than three children to care for and a house to clean, among other things. The child is given a dime with a hole put through it with a nail to wear around their neck. For a boy, the dime must come from an aunt, and for a girl it has to come from an uncle in order for it to have its "charm." To ease the discomfort, Mama would also rub our gums with a silver thimble placed on her ring finger, said to be the best for applying medicine and prayer. A deer-tooth necklace also helps with teething, as does a necklace made of strung elderberries, dried and dipped in the creek on Easter morning.

These stories and tricks are passed down in families and communities, routinely offered as wives'-tale cures, or simple reminiscing of things that helped folks get along in their daily life. We have a good helping of these stories to tell should you ever make your way down to these mountains. The tea is always made and, Lord willing, it'll be a good day to sit on the porch in one of the wicker rocking chairs.

So now that you know how we think, how open we are to the presence of the unknown, and the bits of wisdom we continue to follow to this day, let's get to work on putting our hands (and feet) to use in doing and working with the forces that run up one side of these mountains and down the other. Go ahead and kick those shoes off: it's time to greet the land you're on. One cannot work the roots of the land, harvest herbs, or converse with the spirits if one is not first acquainted with the soil that's home to it all. The soil beneath your feet is the firmament of this work, and you need to know it.

3

BAREFOOT WANDERING
Connecting with the Land

n this chapter, you will learn how to connect with the land in a down-home manner unique to this work. These teachings weren't learned or taught by the old folks. It was just what they did and how they lived that kept them close to the rhythms and seasons of these hills, often indirectly. As the Southern Highlands become more modernized with clinics and hospitals, fast-food joints, and grocery stores in every town, those growing up in the city often have a blurry connection to nature. Many people today go their whole lives without digging in the soil or playing in the creeks.

No longer do the cracks in the woodwork of homes need stuffing with newspaper in the winter to keep the cold out. No longer is timber needed to heat the home or boil water. As a culture we were born from this soil, and we have traded it over to the coal and oil companies. We sold our soil, our soul, for an industrial entertainment with the hopes of a growing economy. Most may not notice, but I do. Our seasons are off, our region-specific species of animals and plants are disappearing or leaving, and our mountains are being gutted for her coal.

Noticing, observing, and knowing one's land intimately also entails protecting it. We've heard the stories and know the history that has painted these hills, but we are not their author. In my lifetime, I have watched countryside be taken over by strip malls and highways. I've watched hills be decimated to make way for another interstate ramp. Some of my local readers may remember the giant beech trees, known as Robert Young's trees, planted by the man himself who played an important role in the Revolutionary War. Those trees have stood in Johnson City on the corner of West Market and State of Franklin since the nineteenth century. But as these hills became more modern, they were cut off at the knee to build something that never happened.

The trees were buried and forgotten. Where five or six giant beings once stood a grave hill was left. Over a decade went by before they built the current strip mall that consists of a grocery store, a Chick-fil-A, and a Walgreens. People were outraged when the trees were cut down; now barely anyone remembers them, let alone the one who planted them.

Knowing the land, and what goes on in it, means knowing the spirit of the place and the people who have lived there. These hills are filled with more history than books can hold; no matter where you stand, your feet rest where someone else's did more than two hundred years ago. Wherever you are, walk outside and ponder what occurred on the spot under your feet. Was someone born there? Did someone die? Maybe there was a reunion of lovers. In Appalachia, the mountains remember everything, and they'll show you how to also. As long as you listen. You may never know the names of those who walked where you do, but that connection lives on in the stones of the earth and the bones in your body. As Mamaw always said, "God gave you two ears and one mouth so you could listen twice as much as you speak."

CONNECTING WITH THE LAND

Go somewhere you know well. Someplace that calls to your bones and stirs your blood, whether that's a forest clearing, a pasture, a church-yard, or a mountain trail. "Betwixt" places such as crossroads, the place where three creeks meet, a river between two mountains, the base of a tree grown into three, or a mountaintop are especially good spots to help bring you "between" times and places. Ponder what took place here. How many footprints do you now follow? How many forgotten graves lay beneath the red clay? How many bones has this soil devoured?

Feel the presence of the place. This is the spirit of the land. While few speak of the spirit as having form, it is likely to appear as an animal, a cluster of summer gnats in the sunlight, or a whisper on the breeze. Those with the sight are more inclined to see them; some have reported the spirit of the land lives in the trees themselves and is a simple voice that speaks from an unknown source, while others say it takes the form of giants that make their residence in the mountaintops or the rocks by the rivers. Many of them are left without a name because, much like this work, they're too old for those things or anyone living today.

When you find where your roots are nourished, give an offering to the land. The Cherokee gave corn, tobacco, and blood. The Irish gave bread, butter, and sweet things. Today's Appalachian workers give tobacco, food, hard candy, whiskey, coins, and old cheap jewelry. Sit with the land and feel your surroundings. Walk about and familiarize yourself with the hills and rocks and trees.

Don't expect them to be accepting of you right away, or at all, really. As with any other friendship, it takes time to become familiar with each other and sometimes it will never grow. Some of these land spirits simply wish to be left alone and unbothered by humans. Who could blame them, after the blood-drenched history they have witnessed in these hills? The spirit of a place is simply someone who has taken up residence on that land, meaning it could be a little person, or a haint, or it could simply be made up of the events that occurred there. For example, a bridge known for suicides wouldn't be a good place to start, as it would contain the spiritual traits of its distinguished events.

It will take many times of showing up, giving an offering, and simply presenting yourself before any presence will be shown. Because not all spirits have your best interest in mind, I'd reckon you ought to carry three used horseshoe nails on you: one around your neck and two under the soles of your shoes. It's quite an odd thing to try and do, but with a handy pocketknife you can pry the soles up just enough to slide a nail under it right at the heels. It may be a bit uncomfortable, but horses have always been regarded in Appalachia as being able to see and protect from haints.

In the spring, take a walk through the woods and note what is growing and flowering. Collect willow fronds and strip the leaves on the front porch. Place them in a jar of water, and set it in direct sunlight without the lid on. This is sun-brewed tea, and you can apply it to wounds and aches. Notice the first animals that are roused by the warming weather.

You'll begin to notice the wave created by the life of the forest. In early spring the first vegetative life returns at the forest floor, and this growth moves upward, from the bloodroot to the honeysuckle bush, from the vines into the trees. In summer, the leaves come to fruition and the flesh of the mountain covers the bones of yesteryear. When fall approaches, life retreats, starting in the treetops and exiting at the forest floor.

The mountain spirit moves through the migration and stillness of the animals through these cycles: geese fly north, bears emerge from old caves, and salamanders make their voyage to the water. Appalachia is continuously alive, continuously surviving and struggling and triumphing. In the fall, walk amongst the fodder of dead corn and pick the silk. These precious "hairs," as Nana calls them, help women with bloating. For children, it makes a great tea to help with bedwetting. Simply wrap a bundle of silk in a coffee filter and steep in barely boiling water for about five minutes.

The fodder of the corn stalks is placed about the home so the family will always have food; radishes and pumpkins are sat on the porch, carved to keep haints away. The forests are on fire with colors of gold and red; it's time to dig the roots and ground crops before the first moon of October so they don't rot.

But it is when you are done pulling the roots, cutting the fodder, and rending the vines from iron trellises, covered in scrapes and itching skin, that you feel the land within you. It is when your hair is drenched with sweat and the sun is beating down on your back that you feel the sting and pride of your ancestors rising in your own skin from the same hard work.

In the winter, find your solace in the coyote howls and your warmth in a big cup of coffee while watching the cardinals pick away the seeds left from the season's sunflowers. Blue jays, cardinals, and blackbirds are just about the only ones left to brave the mountain winters. The only food in storage is cabbage, beans, and canned whatnots from the last harvest.

A blanket of snow has covered everything from the previous year, and we soon forget what the sun feels like until spring. When the warmth returns, when the blood of beasts begins to rush again, go down to the river and pray. The mountain has awoken. The trees begin their upward triumph into greenery and another year of work has begun.

The Cherokee believed that every animal was our brother or sister and that God gave us plant medicines to help us care for our bodies and spirits. Many families here continue to hold this worldview. Since Appalachia is one of the most biodiverse regions in the country, with over ten thousand species of animals and plants recorded so far, it's natural that the mountain critters and foliage would have a strong influence on the mind, faith, and medicine here.

Many people I know start picking dandelions in the spring when they first arise to make them into jams, while others wait for the autumn elderberries to turn the dark berries into syrups and drink. I pick cattail root throughout the year for wounds, burns, bee stings, and toothache.

Before making any kind of remedy, Nana always made sure the Lord was involved through reciting either of these two Psalms:

> O LORD my God, I cried unto thee, and thou hast healed me.
>
> *Psalm 30:2*

> I waited patiently for the LORD; and he inclined unto me and heard my cry.
>
> *Psalm 40:1*

She'd also say how she was grateful the corn grew "mighty high" this year. Food was an important thing in our home, and many superstitions arose around it and the kitchen. Women who are on their flow or in menopause weren't supposed to cook certain things aside from good meat and broth, otherwise they'd spoil the food and it wouldn't turn out.

Becoming familiar with the land one resides on also entails learning about it. Study the indigenous herbs, trees, and animals that are scattered throughout these hills. Learn their medicine to use them safely in remedies. Don't learn just through books, either. Grow and harvest the plants yourself, or find them out in the woods and fields. Grind their sticks and roots with a grindstone or mortar and pestle to see them transform into medicine.

Speak with your elders about how they worked and healed through the land. They have witnessed the turn of many seasons and are a valuable source of wisdom.

HONEST WORK

You will never be able to build relationships through books or other people alone. Your connection to the land under your feet resides in your blood. The blood that runs through my veins has raced through those of my ancestors as they tilled the soil and pushed the plow. The power of relationships in Appalachia is built through honest work and good food. It's built with family and love, and it's an integral part of our culture.

It's winter in East Tennessee as I write this, and Christmas is soon on its way. The puttyroot is long gone and the deer are scavenging in the field across the road. There's a vulture pair living in one of the high trees behind the field, a tree close to its end. The cold wind is blowing and the vultures have their wings spread to get warm in the sun.

This morning I found an old corn necklace that was handed down to me. Red corn kernels are worn to help with fevers and bleeding. Lord knows how long ago that corn was grown and strung or how many necks it has hung from. The kernels are now ancient and brittle. Some have fallen off, while others have cracked down the center and seem to be hanging on by their last thread. One wrong, heavy step on the floorboards would surely release them and send them flying.

It was honest work that grew that corn. It was honest faith that strung the kernels together. It was love that passed it down through the family. This medicine and magic were grown in warm isolation. Isolated due to the mountains and poverty, but warm because of the family and love it grew under. Today, it thrives on the memory of grandparents long gone, good days gone by, and proud, honest work. You'll never fill their shoes nor have the faith they did with this work. We live in different times and practically a different world than they did. Needs have changed. After me, that necklace may never be worn again.

Mamaw's old charms for when the cows go dry no longer apply to the world today, so they will remain in her recipe box as they always have, among other things. A graveyard of charms, so to speak. Mad-stones aren't used anymore to draw poison out, as Western medicine is readily available for snakebites and rabies, so mine will rest in the chester drawers. Folks only want the things this work can offer to help satisfy their desires. Screw the burn, nightmares, or cough. Society has conditioned us to deal with these and keep going. These things are no longer what they used to be for our ancestors years ago, when a simple cough could lead to a slow, fatal sickness or a burn could cause gangrene.

While there's nothing wrong with fulfilling desires, or bringing about change, it's still sad that certain works need to retire. But we still deal with the same battles of food insecurity, poverty, bad luck, unemployment, and more. Though we don't rely on the survival of crops now because we have grocery stores, and we don't resort to folk remedies because we have access to medical services, we need to realize how we'd do without those things like the old folks did. We can relate and romanticize that time all we want, but it still won't help bring this work into today's age.

So, make an effort to relate to their struggles, learn all you can about their lives and those time periods. Many of my ancestors died from illnesses that are easily curable today such as the common cold, fever, or infections. Learn the stories of your family and relate to them. Doing so will teach you to have humility and pride in your heritage. I cannot teach you these things, especially through a book, but I can tell you that humility is the most important thing in this work. Nana has never said that it is she who does this work or has the power. All the power comes from God. Even when someone has the sight, it's not them or theirs; it's God alone who gives it and powers it.

So be honest in this work, with yourself and the spirits. Go to the fields and forests. Go treasure hunting. Go put your feet in the water and listen to the wind chimes as the minnows nibble at your toes. Till the soil, align the rows, sift the stones from the dirt, and plant the seeds. Over time you will know the land and it will know you. It may take a while, but I can say, for sure as I've been stomping through creeks and woods my whole life, your bones will root themselves in the soil eventually. Just be honest and curious about it all. The best things are found through curiosity. Coincidentally, those are the same things that are cherished for a lifetime.

CLAIMING YOUR ROOTS

The best and most fulfilling way to connect to the land is to find your own roots scattered throughout it. Learn about your ancestral lands, the places your family has resided. Finding the childhood home of a great-grandparent can ignite your bones with moonshine and make your heart feel like a worn patchwork quilt. It's almost indescribable to be standing where your ancestors did, right on the soil where they were brought up.

My family on both sides has lived in Appalachia for quite a while. From Virginia and Tennessee to the Carolinas, they've farmed this land, dug the mines, and forged the metal in these mountains for well on three hundred years. To find out about your own ancestry, start at home. Ask your elders to tell you stories about their parents, where they grew up, and what they went through. If you don't have relative elders living, ask your older neighbors. Things may have changed drastically since then, but with some determination it is easy to relate to those trials if you're from the same area. I'll tell you one of my stories.

My great-great-grandmother, Myra Tipton, was kicked out of the local Baptist Church. Back in those days, it was not fit for a woman to wear a man's hat aside from during labor, which was done to give the woman support and the strength of the man who wore it (usually her husband). Women were expected to wear bonnets, especially in the Lord's house. Well, Mamaw didn't care much for those rules. Every Sunday, as she was walking home from church, she'd take off her bonnet and take out the hat she had concealed beneath her dress and put it on till she got home. One day, the preacher and her father, Sidney, saw her make the exchange and kicked her out of the church. She was told the only way she could come back was to stand before the congregation and beg forgiveness from them and from God. Needless to say, Mamaw became a Methodist.

I cherish this story, as it shows the ruthless truth and stubbornness of the Tipton family that runs in my blood. My Mamaw Sadie, my mother's mother, was also a brave woman. She never stepped down from no one, and plenty of the family feared her when she was angry. She was four feet tall and full of hot temper. One time, a drunk man threatened Mamaw Sadie, saying he was going to get his gun. She retorted, "Go get your gun, you bench-legged bastard. I'll show you how to use it." She was no flower or peach, to say the least. She was a wonderful woman with bones of burning coal and a rod of iron for a backbone. Her strength and fearlessness live on in the family still, as well as the gifts from her side of the family.

Stories and tales keep us humble and honest and close to the home as long as we listen to them. They paint portraits on the soil we sit on, watching the teller in awe as he gives life to each character, bridging worlds, and moving mountains. It was always a joy when one of the grandparents told a story, especially when it was one of the old ones handed down generations. Held close, family stories are tucked right in the heart pocket and carried for the rest of your life. Thankfully, my heart is big enough for all of those carried by my elders for generations. This leads us into the next part of this work, which is also one of the most important. It acts like a creek from heaven flowing through the past, right into you here and now, and back into the future. It is the bones and dirt of these tales I'm recalling. The place the stories all come from. The ancestors.

4

SOUP BEANS AND CORNBREAD
Ancestor Veneration

Have mercy, soup beans and cornbread are a timeworn dish that always satisfies when you're not sure you want anything else. It's a favorite of my family and many others going back generations. It is the poor man's dish for anytime, breakfast, lunch, or supper. It's served often with stewed or fried potatoes and maybe some boiled cabbage. In old Appalachia, this dish was a staple because the beans and corn lasted well into the winter and helped folks get by during hard times.

A good majority of the culture in Appalachia involves food that's readily available: ham, bacon, corn, fried squash, pickled okra, cornbread, green beans, potatoes, deer meat, and more. Whether it's at a family reunion, a funeral, a marriage, a grave decoration, or simply on a warm summer's night when all the family or neighbors would often get together and have dinner, food is at the center of Appalachia culture.

Food is as important to our heritage as the stories passed down to us. Our food is the embodied struggle and poverty of our people, but it is also the love and pride we take in ourselves and in our upbringing. It is comfort for our grief and a sign of hospitality and comradery in our communities and in the seams of our family history.

Often the food itself tells a tale. Every Thanksgiving, my Papaw Trivett made chicken and dumplings; every fall, my Mamaw Margie would make her famous pumpkin pie; and my Mamaw Hopson was always making biscuits with apple butter, no matter the season or the weather. Years later, these recipes remain in cold tin and wooden boxes sat lovingly by the stove.

The memory of the dead in Appalachia is somewhat based around the foods and drinks they loved in their lifetime. One cannot think about their loved ones without also remembering what they enjoyed. So, we recreate it in their honor; sometimes in an attempt to recreate those memories, although nothing could hold a candle to the foods they made in life. On the birthdays and other anniversaries of our dead, we often prepare their favorite dishes with a prayer that they accept what we've made of the recipes they left and that they're enjoying it in heaven. Many families continue a tradition of leaving a space at the table for their dead. Food may or may not be placed on their plate, depending on the family.

THE GRAVEYARD

Food is especially important in the little-known tradition of Decoration Day, which consists of the family getting together and eating before heading to the family cemeteries to dress, clean, and decorate the graves of the familiar dead. The graves of the children are tended to first, and then those of the elders. Flowers, plates of food, toys for the children, liquor, and cigarettes are often left on the graves. In Appalachia, this isn't seen as odd or in the least bit pagan; it's common sense and manners. It doesn't matter if someone's dead or not—you never eat, drink, or smoke in front of someone without offering them some, especially if you know they like it as well.

After the graves of the family are honored, we move over to the graves with worn, indiscernible inscriptions and wash them, pick up debris nearby, and lay flowers down. We always take extra flowers for the forgotten dead. We also make sure to go around and read off the names and dates of every stone while offering a moment of prayer after each. It's not something that's taught, nor is there some ritualistic reason behind it. It's simply what the old folks did.

If ever someone comes by my future grave, long after I've been forgotten, I would like for them to wonder who I was, what I went through, and maybe what now-indiscernible name was there. No one wants to be forgotten, especially the mountaineer, and, God forbid, especially by his own people. Although it takes time and effort to go to each gravesite, these visits to the dead are always looked forward to.

DEATH AND DYING

Death and the dead have created a big impact in the folk magic and beliefs of these hills, calling to the fact Death takes our loved ones away and the passing of those sometimes ended the survival of a family, especially if it was the breadwinner of the house. Behind the gravestones, hymns such as "In the Sweet By and By," and upbeat religious ceremonies of Appalachian funerals filled with promises of going home to that golden country, there lives a thread of superstition and fear when it comes to visits from Death and the bodies of those taken.

The oldest traditions of washing and burying the dead are no longer, but it wasn't long ago that the dead were tied to the cooling board and swaddled in a shroud; this practice was as recent in my family as three generations ago. At the moment of death, the local church bell was rung for each year the person lived, announcing their passing in the community. Everything stopped when the bell rang; people bowed their heads and prayed, while others gave a moment of silence or ran crying to the home. The number of tolls helped folks figure out who had passed, and the news spread fast; by evening the house was filled with relatives and neighbors who'd come to offer food and help to the family in their mourning.

Care of the body was important, but the burden was sometimes spared from the immediate family—other close family members or neighbors would take care of the arrangements. And sometimes the whole family sat up with the dead, talking about the person into the night with laughter and tears.

Upon death, the body was washed and dressed quickly, as there was no way to preserve the body long. Women washed women and men washed men for the simple taboo that you shouldn't see the nakedness of someone who isn't your spouse. Oftentimes the body was dressed in flowers, if they were available, to mask any smells that may arise from the deceased. After being dressed, the body was laid on the cooling board, which could be an old ironing board or a slab of wood that was usually passed down in the family. The chest and feet were tied to the board to prevent the body from rising and a bowl of unmixed salt and earth was placed on the chest to prevent swelling and to keep the Devil away. Sometimes a simple bag of salt was tied around the neck for the same purpose.

Next, two pieces of silver money, usually quarters or half-dollars, are placed on the eyes to prevent them from opening. Pennies weren't used because copper tended to turn the skin green. This is the origin of the phrase, "he'd steal money from a dead man's eyes." The coins are also used for the age-old belief that you should enter heaven with your eyes closed. This shows the Lord that you see yourself unworthy to enter and that you beg forgiveness for your sins. Plus, I reckon open eyes on a corpse is just plain creepy.

The body was then buried within three days, but was never kept over Sunday. To do so meant another death would occur in the house that year. So if the person passed on Friday, the body would be buried the next day. The body was also not to be taken out of the house head-first; otherwise, their spirit would either haunt the home or beckon another family member to the grave. The body is always carried out feetfirst. (Strangely, it is the opposite when the body is carried into the church: it must be carried in headfirst to keep the spirit from haunting the house of the Lord.) The windows and doors were left open to let the spirit out, and oftentimes they remained that way until after the funeral. Another custom to keep the dead from returning was to change the doorknob and deadbolt of the front door or rearrange the furniture.

After church, the body was carried by mule and wagon to the cemetery—it was never to pass over running water—and the wagon always stopped at any crossroads along the way to let the dead catch up.

The dead were usually buried in hollowed-out logs that had the top piece removed until burial. These soon evolved into simple pinewood boxes that were often made free of charge by neighbors or friends. The coffin was oftentimes draped with a black cloth and lined with cotton or linen.

The digging of the grave was an important rite in itself, full of faith and superstition. The weather is often read while digging the grave. One old saying goes, "blessed is the dead it rains onto." Others say when it rains, the soul of the dead is happy; the rain helps the family through grief, and it's a sign the soul is going to heaven since the vault has opened to let the rain down. However, it was bad luck for it to rain into an empty grave. The treatment of the grave before it was occupied also held important power to foretell another death or bring misfortune. It was never left open overnight or over Sunday, and the digging never started before sunrise of the day the corpse was to be buried. Burials were often held in the evening, as the sun was setting.

If the diggers' shovels clink together while digging, there will be another death soon; and if the filled grave sinks after a period of days, it is making way for another member of the family. Signs like these were always heeded in the hills, and they've stuck for generations. If a bad storm happens soon after the burial, then it is a sign that the deceased isn't at peace. The first person to leave the cemetery after a burying foretells the next death: if a man leaves first, the next death will be a man and vice versa if it's a woman.

Direction plays an important part in a lot of our tales and tricks, especially with the dead. The dead were buried as Christ was, with their head to the west, so they could see Jesus coming from the east at Judgment Day. Also, many folks today still make sure their plot is running east to west and will do everything possible to avoid having to be buried in one that runs north to south, as that's the way witches were buried, and it's said that's the path the Devil ran.

After burying the body, young ones dress the grave with flowers from the home. The tools that were used to dig the plot are left there for three days in the form of a cross to help ease the spirit of the deceased and sanctify the grave. Along with the crossed tools, a lantern or candle was sometimes left on the freshly stirred soil to "lead 'em on to glory," as Nana said. Some folks would even take home a handful of the dirt or a flower from the grave to let the dead know they won't be forgotten. A lot of care was used in tending the dead, pre- and post-mortem. Throughout the whole process, they were loved and honored, lifted with the prayer and strength of their families up to the Lord.

Today, Appalachia has conceded to handing the care of the body and funeral arrangements over to corporations and the authorities. However, in our case it was very reluctant and didn't occur until the twentieth century—and as late as the 1950s in some areas. Funerals aren't as personal as they once were; barely any time is given for the families at the burial, and the family is cut off completely from the care of the body between the bed and the grave. Some states have since made laws allowing the family to care for their dead, but they are in the minority so far.

COMMUNING WITH THE DEAD

All year we pray and talk with our ancestors, their plates are set at dinner, and we remember them in the stories we hold in our hearts.

Sometimes we see them around us, at home or in town. We've often seen my Papaw Trivett walking up the hallway of the house. It's mostly just a glimpse of the flannel shirts he used to wear, but we know it's him by the smell of his Old Spice cologne. Other times, my grandmother has said she saw her daddy in a dream or her mama moseying around in the kitchen. Sometimes these are the ghosts of the dead, meaning they haven't moved on. Others times, they are simply letting us know they are still with us in spirit.

The love and honor we give our ancestors is instilled in us at a young age. You never speak ill of the dead, walk over a grave, or dismiss their presence in your life. Some folks like to imagine them as guardian angels, and that's quite alright. Some families create shrines for their ancestors. Whether it's a place on the mantle, an old vanity, or a bookshelf, folks often keep photos and keepsakes of the dead. These shrines are usually in the living room of the home and are always adorned in white cloth, doilies, or lace. I've never seen one in black. My grandmother has a spot in her living room for my Papaw Trivett. His photos are hung on the wall and some of his things are set on her vanity. His old handkerchiefs and prayer cloths, his obituary, and the printed poem from his funeral are tenderly set beside a painted porcelain cross with prayer beads on it. His wedding ring sits in a jewelry box.

My own shrine is a bookshelf in my living room set with mugs of water and whiskey alongside photos of my grandparents and great-grandparents and some of their belongings. I have my Papaw John's whittling knife; my Mamaw Hopson's old remedy book and Bible; and my Papaw Trivett's Indian Head penny, bolo tie, and old cast-iron work hammer. I also have a shard of old Cherokee pottery to represent my Cherokee grandmother, Sieomi. Their photos are lovingly decked with lace and rosemary, anointed with oil every week, and smudged with tobacco smoke.

Many workers follow certain taboos in ancestor veneration, such as keeping photos of the living off the altar and only having photos of blood relatives there. The former is true in Appalachia as well, but the latter never took root, as many of us include friends and neighbors as family. I have my step-grandfather John on my altar. He was there when I was born and loved me until he died, so I consider him family—and my children will as well, regardless of blood connection. Another taboo some follow is to never put salt on an altar, as the ancestors apparently hate it. Not here. We put salt in every food we eat, so every dish we offer the ancestors also has salt in it. They've never complained with us.

In order to do this work, you will need to build a relationship with your ancestors. Ask your living relatives about them; learn their stories, their achievements, and their setbacks. This is especially helpful if you didn't know them in life, as you will be able to relate to them through the stories. Set up an altar to them. This not only makes a place for them in your home, but in your life as well. You will be aware of them and their presence every time you pass it.

Set out a white cloth or lace and place their photos on it. Set a dish aside for their food alone. I keep a candy dish on my shelf for the chocolates and cinnamon candies my grandparents loved. Place a couple glasses of water, a candle, and other things they enjoyed in life. Maybe that's a tin of snuff, a pack of cigarettes, a shot of their preferred liquor, old dolls, or other items that once belonged to them. Arrange these according to your own feeling, praying from the heart as you do so.

Most workers dedicate a certain day of the week to honor their ancestors and refresh their water and other offerings. I chose Sunday, as it is traditionally the day for prayer and rest in the south, but choose whichever day you feel is best. On that day you offer your ancestors prayers and love, but it is also the time for you to just talk to them. Remember out loud fond memories from your childhood with them, tell them how much they are missed and loved. Mourn their loss if you're still in that stage. Tell them how your day went, what troubles you, and what is uplifting you. Don't feel that you're talking too much or bothering them, because you're not. It's like a phone call from a relative you haven't heard from in ages.

Don't worry if you don't always feel their presence. Sometimes they won't be around, but it's not because they don't love you. It's not a telephone service, and they won't always answer. God just didn't intend for that.

My ancestors only show up and speak to me directly when it's important. Other times, I simply keep my faith and love for them wrapped close together. Mama taught me the beloved dead might not always speak to you when you want because if they did, it would blur the line between the living and the dead. They died for a reason, greater than you or them. Also, it just isn't good for the mind.

Another possibility, if you believe in reincarnation, as I do, is that some of your folks may already be in another life. However, the vast majority of Appalachian doctors and grannies were Christians, so they believed the dead were either already up on high or sleeping in the grave awaiting Judgment Day. The belief varies based on the church and region. So, if Mamaw doesn't show up or make her presence known, it's probably for good reason, whether that's incarnation in another life, sleeping in the grave, or simply staying quiet for the time being. Or maybe you should just pay closer attention.

I mentioned earlier the practice of washing away the sins of the blood in regards to our ancestors' acts of slavery, war, rape, etc. Among the "sins" are the traumas they went through that have spiraled down in the family, such as alcoholism, suicide, divorce, abuse, and gambling addiction. We have a duty to them, because it is in their stories that ours begin. Their stories may have begun in suffering, poverty, and sin, but through us they can end with healing, stability, and salvation. We can break the blood-born chains that kept them down and that have the power to take us down as well, unless we act.

There's a very strong belief in generational chains and curses in Appalachia; but the majority have nothing to do with witchcraft, but rather with the mind and spirit. Many of us have battled depression and suicidal thoughts. A handful of my ancestors have committed suicide. In my own life, I broke that chain early in my commitment to live. I stopped self-harming, stopped dwelling on that part of my family history, and started enjoying life.

Figure it out in your own blood. What secrets, troubles, or sins lurk within your family tree? Talk to your elders. Back in the day, some things weren't spoken of. Families would literally cut themselves off from a relative because of something they wouldn't speak of for years. Sometimes that silence between folks lasted to the grave, and I'm sure it still happens all too often.

Folks have offered differing meditations for this kind of work, but I couldn't find good soil in them. If you think you can, then I suggest you look into it further. As this writing is of my own family practices and experiences, I can only offer this: pay attention to the family stories, to your dreams, and to your own behavior. The bad root under it all will show itself in time. Maybe there are hints lingering in your childhood memories. Maybe it's something you'd rather not speak about. Take it to the ancestors. They already know, and they're willing to help. Oftentimes, these sins that live on are the things holding them here and keeping them from peace.

Our ancestors protect us and comfort us from the other side. They can be a part of your life, to both celebrate with and cry with. Listen to them with your whole heart. During your daily life, pray to them. There's not a day that goes by that I do not love and honor the makers of the footprints on my path. They have made the way with their sweat and tears, which has made our lives considerably easier. We owe them our memory and love and respect. In return, they are our biggest comfort and our strongest shield.

I've heard of folks who have bad dealings with some of their dead, and it's almost always due to that bad root in the blood. Know this: you don't have to call up a person you had a contentious relationship with if you're not ready. In your prayers, tell your ancestors you do not wish for "Jane Doe" to be present because of certain reasons. The spirits will understand this and will not push you further unless conciliation is needed.

Often, these are the dead that will come to you in dreams, smells, memories, and more. This is them wishing to connect with you, to often make amends, and more. You are not obligated to concede, but you do need to acknowledge them and forgive. The primary thing that holds the dead back is unfinished business, cliché as it may sound.

This needs to be mentioned: being dead doesn't make a person a saint, suddenly enlightened, or better than they were. The dead come back to us as they were in life, and they will exemplify this when you work with them. If they were mean and hateful in life, they'll be the same in death. If they were kind and gentle, they'll be the same. Bad branches of the family tree can still have a negative effect on you and the fruit you try to grow.

It is important to know the spirits you're calling up, even among your ancestors. When tending to their altar or going to them for something, I always knock on the table three times (manners) and ask them to show in the name of the Father, the Son, and the Holy Ghost. By that name, no evil or darkness may approach. You may also want to clean the altar once in a while with a wash of vinegar, whiskey, and church dust. This is the root of your family tree, and your shrine is the garden where it's planted. Nourish that tree, but at the same time focus on finding the bad root that has plagued it. Your life will be better for acknowledging it and for doing the work to heal it; and your ancestors will be at peace knowing that their blood and sins are on the mend, and they can rest.

5

FROM THE EAST, FROM THE WEST
Living by Signs and Omens

t was that wild medicine, the health of the crops in the field, and the
wisdom handed down from generations that decided the survival
and prosperity of the little mountain communities. An early frost, a
bad blight, or planting during the wrong sign could endanger the entire
harvest. So certain measures were devised to prevent misfortunes of
this type.

Omens and lore surround the act of planting, growing, caretak-
ing, and harvesting mainly for the purpose of health and life. The
major belief in omens and signs comes from the Bible, Ecclesiastes
3:1–2: "Let there be lights in the firmaments of the heavens to divide
the day from the night; and let them be for signs, and for seasons, and
for days, and years." This led the old folks to believe that just about
everything had its appointed time, whether it was a certain moon
phase to cut your hair or even the best day to get married. One mistake could result in death, with the case of an old saying, "If a row of
corn is unknowingly left unplanted, death will visit the family before
harvest." To prevent this, that last row must be planted before the
other rows sprout from the ground or before the first sunset after
finding the unplanted row. Things were done based on what sign

the moon was in, and each sign was associated with a body part, its government over man's affairs.

SETTING OUT

Follow these guidelines when you go to set out the seed or go hunting:

- Plant peas and other crops that produce multiples when the sign is in the arms (Gemini). However, never plant green beans at this time, as they'll bloom themselves to death and won't bear anything worthwhile.

- Always plant corn when the sign is in Leo, which is associated with the heart. Under Leo, it will grow tall and be less prone to blight or bugs.

- The heart and chest (Cancer) is the best sign for fast germination.

- Plant flowers in the sign of the "posy girl" (Virgo), as this causes plants to flower a lot but bear little fruit. (Virgo is the worst sign to plant food under, especially since it's associated with the bowels.) Hunt deer when the sign is in Virgo because they will be slow to scare—and never hunt under the sign of the legs (Aquarius) or the thighs (Sagittarius).

- Cut flowers when the sign is in the head (Aries) to keep the blooms from wilting too fast. This is also a good time to catch fish.

- Fish won't bite at all when under the sign of the feet (Pisces).

  When it comes to textiles, follow these guidelines:

- Get wool that has been freshly sheered from the sheep or goat when the moon is in the head (Aries).

- Wash the fiber when it's in the chest (Cancer).

- Card the wool into roving and dye it when the sign is in the legs (Aquarius) for the best results.

Ailments of a body part where also more vulnerable or easily hurt during its own sign. For example,

- You're more apt to get a sore throat when the moon is in the sign of the neck, Taurus.

- The knees ache most when the sign is in Capricorn.

- Kidney stones are hardest to pass when the sign is in Libra, the reins.

Finally, one more piece of advice for good measure: never tell secrets or have flirtatious affairs during the sign of Scorpio, or your secrets may well be exposed.

We also pay attention to the direction of the wind and its effects as it blows from a particular direction. If you sow seeds while the wind is blowing from the north or northeast, they won't sprout at all—and if they do, they will be more vulnerable to being fried by the sun. If you sow seeds when the wind is in the east, bugs will destroy the yield. Wind from the west or south ensures good growth. There are a few sayings about east winds in the mountains, to help you remember: "Wind in the east isn't good for man or beast." In regards to fishing, "Wind in the east, the fish bite least; wind in the west, the fish bite best; and wind in the south, the fish bite with the mouth." The last phrase means the fish will bite on the hook instead of just the bait.

This part of Appalachian lore is odd, because the east is usually a favored direction for good things in many aspects. But I do remember my Papaw John's sunflowers struggling after he sowed the seeds when the wind was out of the east. They were eaten up with ants and little white mites. When the seeds were taken out and examined, there were holes plumb through them all. There are many, many more examples of beliefs like these—far too many to place in this chapter or this book— but here's a starting place for you should you decide to take up the seed by the moon and head out to the garden.

Both of my grandmothers had huge gardens complete with toma- toes, squash, corn, green beans, sunflowers, and cabbage. They were well versed by the signs and weather wisdom their mamas taught them. These gardens, along with the meat brought home from hunting and fishing, often constituted half or more of their food even with grocery stores around the corner. It was cheaper to pay the hunting license fee and plant your own seeds—and faith and prayer are always free. There was always a large storage of canned goods containing everything from the garden. Many of the jars held dates showing when they were canned, always with a thin layer of dust on the lids from the shed they were stored in.

Plants and animals have long sustained the body of the mountain- eer in Appalachia, from filling bellies to healing wounds. A plethora of books have been written on the medicinal uses of native and exotic herbs, but nothing has been compiled regarding the superstitious doings behind the herbs and their care. "There's a time for everything by the Word. There's a time to plant, there's a time to work, there's a time to dig wells. It's all in the Bible," as my Nana explained. And from what I've seen, this holds true.

Plants and crops that bear their fruit above ground are always planted in the "change of the moon," when the moon is moving from new to full. Root crops such as carrots, ginger, and potatoes are planted when the moon is changing from full to new, in its waning phase. If root crops are planted when the moon is waxing, they'll simply vine themselves all over and the crops will either be very small or they won't come at all. Same with the above ground crops: if they're planted in the waning of the moon, there won't be much growth aside from the deep, useless roots they'll put down into the earth.

When planting crops, herbs, or flowers, my family always faces the east, because that's where Christ is believed to be coming from and he is the "bread of life," symbolizing that all good food comes from that auspicious direction. Facing east, we make a hole with a stick into the soil. As we're placing the seeds into the holes, we sing a planting tune:

> *Some for the birds and some for I,*
> *some for the beetle and some for the fly.*
> *Some to rot and some to grow,*
> *Lord, bless these seeds I now do sow.*

I imagine the symbolism of the bird, beetle, and fly is calling for good germination and pollination for another generation of the seed for harvest. It was also to offer a bit of the bounty to those called up in the rhyme in order to keep away thievery on the part of the bird, beetle, and fly by offering them their due up front.

Another little rhyme we were taught was done while planting watermelons, radishes, carrots, and more:

> *As long as my arm, as thick as my leg;*
> *as round as my ass, and as big as my head.*

We were telling the crops to be big and bountiful by comparing the vision of its fruit to our limbs or body parts. This was somewhat common back in the day but has decreased in its use along with the practice of following the signs the moon moves through.

GROWING CHARMS

Different techniques were utilized to protect the crops from disease, pests, witches, frost, drought, and other threats. To prevent crops from being killed by the blight, a small tile is placed at each corner of the field plus one in the center, symbolizing the five wounds of Christ. To bring rain during a drought, farmers used to kill a black snake and hang it on a fence or tree limb belly-up. Rain was said to arrive within three days from then. This charm is derived from Europe, although the Cherokee adopted a version of it as well.

Another way to call up rain was to take a handful of pine needles and corn kernels out to the center of the field. Carry them in a white handkerchief on a Monday at noon and face west, because that's where the storms come from, according to the Word of God.

Recite 1 Kings 18:1:

> *Now it happened after many days that the word of the Lord came to Elijah in the third year, saying, "Go and show yourself to Ahab, and I will send rain on the face of the earth."*

Or Jeremiah 10:13:

> *When He utters His voice, there is a tumult of waters in the heavens, And He causes the clouds to ascend from the ends of the earth; He makes lightning for the rain, and brings out the wind from His storehouses.*

Then open the bundle and let the needles and kernels sprinkle down, like gentle rain. I prefer to set a good-sized rock underneath, as the sound is even clearer. Done three Sundays in a row, the rain will usually come within the last week.

The last recipe to conjure rain requires a cat. There's an age-old superstition that a cat is conjuring up a rainstorm when it washes its face. So what did the mountaineer do? He got it to wash its face! Usually a glob of bacon grease, butter, or ice cream was smudged on a cat's nose or cheek for them to wash off. They'd get the cat to wash its face at least three times that day, and it's said rain would come three days after.

If you've ever tended a garden, you understand the pain and frustration felt when pests invade. For this, my Nana would mix up some soapy water and spray around the base of the plant. She would then sprinkle a mixture of cinnamon, tobacco, and cornstarch around her flowers. (The tobacco also deters rabbits and deer.) To help flowers grow, she'd pour the blood from meat into the soil, right at the root of the plant. She'd also take leftover scraps of meat, such as the tough cartilage, and bury that at the root as well.

My great-grandfather John would spread manure in the fields when the horns of the moon pointed downward, usually apparent when the new moon shows over the horizon. This ensured the manure would settle in the soil and enrich it. If this was done when the horns pointed up, the manure would remain at the top all year. Many folks till the fields during winter for a good crop. Jonesborough, Limestone, and Telford are filled with tobacco and cornfields, with a couple of tomato farms here and there as well. Driving by, you can always see dark, freshly tilled soil right around February.

TO SOW IS TO REAP

When harvesting, we gather the plants and fruits in a basket that is lined with white fabric, especially if the plants will be used for medicine. Every time I go to harvest a plant for medicine or work, I face the east at the fourth plant I find and say a prayer telling God what it will be used for, asking for a blessing for the endeavor at hand. I then hold the plant with my left hand and cut with my right, always *receiving* with my nondominant hand. Same when taking a whole plant up or getting the roots. My spirits also advise me to pay attention to things when I go to harvest from the wild or from the garden, such as the activities of animals, the direction of the wind, and the condition of the plant I come upon. Doves, cardinals, and swallows are good signs, being associated with superstitions of good luck; crows, owls, vultures, and whip-poor-wills are bad signs, and more frequently feared for their associations with death, accidents, and illness.

Also pay close attention to the growth of the plant itself when harvesting, especially when digging up roots. When I pull up roots and bulbs, if the roots are knotted or rotting, it's a sign the work will be ineffective; if the roots are smooth and healthy, it will work.

Some plants, such as morning glories, have gnarly roots, so the opposite is true for them: gnarly is good, and slim, straight roots are bad. The formula will usually specify which parts of the plant are needed, but sometimes the entire plant is required. In this case, the plant is pulled up and a piece of bread, a bead, or some cornmeal or tobacco is dropped into the hole as an offering. If the plant's roots show a bad outcome, simply replant it and water it.

If you are taking leaves, flowers, fruit, or bark, pay attention to the toughness of the plant. Oftentimes the spirits will redirect you. You can tell this is happening when the plant refuses to give up any more: you start harvesting leaves easily but then it becomes tougher. When this happens, it's time to stop. You have what you need. Scientifically, this occurs in many species of plants as a defense mechanism against being harvested or eaten by animals to death. An easy harvest is a good sign, but a struggle at the start is a bad sign for the work and a message to reevaluate the situation. I also believe it means you might not yet know everything you need to for the work.

When wildcrafting, most folk hold true to the Cherokee practice of passing the first four to seven plants you find, in order to leave plenty for future generations. After harvesting only what you need or what the spirits limit you to, give an offering of cornmeal or tobacco. These are the tithes we give to the spirits in return for their favor.

Place your harvested portions on your handkerchief or in your basket and don't let it touch the ground. If all other signs up to now are pointing to a good outcome, I sometimes rely on one last method simply for good measure: I will take a bundle of straw, plantain leaves, or tobacco leaves down to the river. This bundle is not tied together with anything. I find a crook in the creek that faces east and hold up the bundle with prayers. I then drop the bundle into the water and watch it. If it separates within three feet as it floats, it foretells failure. If it remains in a loose bundle for nine feet or more as it drifts away, it shows the working or medicine will be a success.

These signs and omens are simply the tip of the iceberg of divinatory practices in Appalachia and only a few that I use in working my roots. I find it customary to always consult a few different methods or signs and look for consistency in the outcome to better understand the direction the spirits point toward.

ROOT AND WEATHER SIGNS

Besides the care taken in planting and harvesting crops, plants were watched for omens. If cabbage grows primarily white leaves, there will be a death soon before it's harvested. If flowers bloom outside of their season, it is also a sign of death. This has always held true for my family. Before my step-grandfather John passed away last winter, the mums outside were blooming out of season in the summer. Before my aunt Marie passed away a few years ago, the irises bloomed through a Christmas blizzard.

Some taboos remain in planting certain plants or trees either on the property or at all. For instance, you're never supposed to plant a willow or walnut tree yourself; otherwise you'll die either when it first blooms or when it's big enough to shade your grave.

We predict the weather by the aches and pains in our body, by the way the wind blows, and by using a jar of animal fat. Aching in the shoulders and arms means it is going to rain a bit; but if the aching is in the back or legs, then there will be a downpour where it's real muddy. There's been many a time that I didn't heed Mama's warnings about the mud and my foot would get stuck; and every time, my shoe was pulled plumb off and just sat there filling with muddy water.

Animal fat or oil shut tight in a jar was left in the window to predict the weather. Often this was duck or bear fat, as it worked better than deer, rabbit, or goose fat. The fat seems to separate in the jar and create layers that are clear, misty, or snowy. If the thickness settles to the very bottom and there's no movement, it foretells nice weather; if it becomes cloudy and the thickness leans a certain way in the jar, it predicts a storm coming from the direction it is leaning.

The activities of animals wild and domestic were also omens. If a black dog howls at night, the Devil is near. If a white dog comes to the home, or follows you home and waits outside, they are waiting for their owner, Death, to visit the home. If a dog crawls on its belly while dragging its hind legs, Papaw always said it was measuring its owner's grave. The same was foretold if you found an inchworm on yourself—expect the worm is measuring you for the death shroud.

YOUR GARDEN

Whether you have a little space outside your home or acres to go with, I encourage you to grow your own food and flowers. Research indigenous herbs and grow them yourself or grow the common sage, vervain, corn, and other crops. If you're going to do a container garden, always make sure the adult plants have enough room to grow deep roots. Otherwise they can and will grow roots through the drain holes and into the ground. This can be a problem with invasive plants, but most others I simply leave like this, as they've technically made themselves at home.

If your garden will be planted in the ground, find good soil. Clay is very hard for most plants to grow in, so you want to find nice brown dirt. Till the soil and make your rows. We always run the rows from east to west, following the path of the sun, for better growth. For some plants like okra, green beans, or morning glories, I recommend using tobacco sticks or metal fence posts if you can find them and drive them deep for good support. Tobacco sticks or thick sticks from the woods can be arranged teepee-style, with the bottoms driven into the ground and the tops bound together with bailing twine or hemp to give these plants something to climb on.

Tomato cages are good for supporting tomatoes as well as cucumbers, peas, and beans. For climbing plants like morning glories, wisteria, or roses, use a trellis or stake. Wisteria becomes woody and very heavy over the years, so it'll need a very strong support that will need to be permanent. You'll sometimes need to tie the stalks of the plant to the pole or cage, in which case you should avoid using wire, twine, or other tight strings because this can harm the plant as the stem grows thicker and sways with the wind. Otherwise you may find your plants decapitated after a big storm. Instead, use strips of old towels or cloth to bind them. I prefer towel strips because the older and more worn they get while outside, the tougher the knot becomes while also allowing the stalk room to grow—but I still go out and loosen the knot once in a while to make more room.

Don't forget our planting song when planting new seeds and making their beds:

> Some for the birds and some for I,
> some for the beetle and some for the fly.
> Some to rot and some to grow,
> Lord, bless these seeds I now do sow.

Here in Appalachia, we plant our seeds on February 14th. Plant yours on a date that you're sure the frost won't kill them (the folklore of other regions may ascribe a different date). This is to swear by if it's done right. It's always best to plant on the even-numbered days of the month, such as the fourth, sixth, eighth, and so on.

However, no matter the number of the day, I never plant anything on a Friday, as I was always told it was bad luck. A lot of things are not to be done on Fridays, such as sewing, spinning, or planting. The consequences range from simple bad luck to dying before your task is ever finished. With planting, the seed will never sprout if it's sowed on a Friday.

The only Friday that is exempt from this prophecy is Good Friday, when the seeds are nourished by the Blood of Christ, ensuring a good yield. If your plants can't be sowed this early in the spring, you can at least make up the garden beds on Good Friday and they'll do just as well. You'll see throughout this work that religious days such as Easter, Ash Wednesday, and Good Friday have a lot of folklore and magic around them. I set out some buckets to collect rainwater as well. I let them get full and water my plants when it's been hot or if it's been about a week since it rained. If the leaves of the plant begin turning yellow or white, pluck them off. This can be an onset of an illness in the plant or a lack of water or too much of it, among other things. This also lets the plant invest just enough energy to heal the place you plucked from compared to a lot of energy spent trying to keep that part alive.

Turn the soil good in your pots every spring before planting. Turn it up so the soil that was at the bottom is primarily at the top for the new year. This will move the majority of the nutrients back to the top. Cover this with new topsoil or manure. So get your spade and tobacco sticks and try your eye at watching the signs for the best growth of your herbs and roots.

6

FOLK RITES OF THE MOUNTAINEER
Techniques and Methods
of the Power Doctor

The people of Appalachia have always clung tightly to the familiarity of their heritage, land, and livelihood, and we easily put up arms when any of these things become threatened in any way. We have routine rituals scattered throughout our lives and land. We cook a certain way, we socialize in particular ways, and we live our daily lives the same. The Appalachian root doctor likewise applies certain techniques and methods to his formulas in repetition and rhythm.

Many of these techniques are simply repeated ways of doing things that show up in different formulas—I call these patterns "rites," as they appear again and again in our folklore. I utilize many rites in my own work, which we'll cover in this chapter. The methods and charms discussed below are also those used by traditional folk healers in Appalachia, namely the hand movements and motions of the fire talkers, thrash throwers, and blood charmers (those who cure burns and thrush, and stop the flow of blood).

PASSING RITES

The act of "passing" is when an object is passed over a person, or the person is passed under or over something for a particular work. Commonly done in blessings, protection work, and cleansings, passing is believed to remove the evil eye, among other things. Passing rites appear in Appalachian lore in a multitude of ways, primarily in those of the Baptist Church, and in the Appalachian funerals, where the candle is passed over the body to bless it. I've performed many blessings on people who come to me helpless, afraid, and afflicted by ill luck. With each one, you can see the stress and worry drain away as the candle is passed over their body and prayers to the Holy Ghost fill the air.

These practices relate to the Bible and the natural world. In the beginning, the Ghost passed over the unformed earth; and that same Spirit is the one who passed over Egypt and brought death, disease, and storms.

In one old remedy for colic, a child is passed backward through a horse collar three times between the parents. In others relating to colic and ailments such as fever or chills, a man and two women (or one woman and two men) are to take the child to a young tree. The tree should be about 10 inches in diameter or "as old as the child." The trunk is split open with an axe or blade, right in the middle, toward the west. In this position, the cutter's back is to the east and he's facing west aligning the cut to run east to west. Once the trunk is split, one person holds the split trunk open while the others pass the child through it three times feetfirst and belly down. Afterward, the trunk is bound back together with rope, and no one is to speak of the event thereafter until the baby outgrows the colic. Working with trees in this manner has also led to the belief that if the tree dies, then the illness will return or the person healed by the tree will likewise die.

Change is effected by leaving the unwanted condition on one side and returning the afflicted to their natural health on the other. This rite appears in many formulas around the world, especially those in Britain and Ireland. I'm sure you're familiar with the large boulders with natural holes weathered into them. Newborns were passed through the holes for health, and sometimes, if the hole was big enough, people would walk right through; a symbolic rebirth.

The numbers of the pass vary, but the general rule is three. As most things in this work, the number three represents the Holy Trinity. Hands are passed over or on the body in faith healing, usually over the head; the same act occurs in many tricks to ease burns or stop blood and in some folk-Baptist deliverance ministries when expelling "demons."

The method of passing is further employed with the use of animals believed to be biblically endowed with power, whether by actual Scripture or the simple folk belief. One formula I continue to follow is using the donkey in my works of healing or protection. In rural Appalachia, donkeys not only kept coyotes and wolves away from cattle and goats, but they also kept the Devil away.

In healing, the donkey is seen as a vehicle for the miraculous power of Christ. This one is actually based on Scripture; others aren't, as most folks couldn't read or write, so they believed what other folks told them about the Good Book and it changed and spread from there. The book of Mark (11:1–10), details the story of Jesus calling for a donkey colt and riding into the city of Jerusalem. He calls specifically for a colt that has never been ridden, which is why the oldest tales say the donkey has to be a colt, but today that isn't always required. After Jesus rode the donkey, its hide was forever marked with a cross.

It is for this reason that the donkey is believed to hold miraculous healing powers. For seizures, sickness, broken bones, and more, a person is passed under and over the donkey nine times, although this is generally only done with children. For adults, they simply crawl under and hop over the donkey nine times. Nine is a very significant number in these charms because Christ died in the ninth hour on the cross, the first battle mentioned in the Bible (Genesis 14:1–2) involved a total of nine kings, and nine is associated with prayer (Acts 3:1 and 10:30).

After the person has been passed, three hairs from their head and four from their toes are taken and placed into some cornbread, which is then fed to the donkey. The use of the donkey in rites of healing or protection stems, to my knowledge, from Ireland and Scotland. There are two other patterns showing in the latter part of this animal charm: transference of disease and what I call "head to toe." Both are explained next.

TRANSFERENCE RITES

Transference rites or "transference of disease" is exhibited in many forms of magic and witchcraft worldwide. It is the belief that things or the essence of them can be transferred from one place or carrier to another. As noted above with the donkey charms, food and hair are fed to an animal with the belief that doing so will pass the affliction from the person to the animal.

Transference takes place in a few forms in Appalachian folk magic. One of these is the creation of a "bag of warts," where a certain number of stones (the same amount as there are warts present) are taken up from the creek and placed in a bag. The bag is left at a crossroads to await the next person who opens it, thereby transferring the warts to them.

A practice for sties says to go to a fork in the road, take up a stone there, and touch it to the afflicted eye while saying, "Sty, sty leave me by; go to the next passerby." This little rhyme is also said while holding a gold wedding ring against the sty. This one I have tried and it works.

All the women from my mother's side of the family treated morning sickness with this practice mentioned earlier: crawling over her husband to get out of bed in the morning. This will pass the symptoms on to him. Sounds cruel, I know, but for some odd reason it didn't hurt them as bad as the women. They get a bit light-headed, nauseated, etc., but that was about it.

Versions of these rites can be found in many forms of magic, especially in the North American folk magic traditions of Appalachia, the Ozarks, the Deep South, and Mexico. Although they are similar, the methods of the mountaineer are unique in the way he utilized his "God-given sense", the land, and the Bible. One of the best examples is that of the egg in Appalachian folk magic. It shows omens and wisdom, and it absorbs and holds tightly the prayers and needs of the user. It can also carry back one's "ghost" after a fright or traumatic event.

"Running the Egg" is one of the cleansing works I use for clients whereby an egg is passed over the client from head to toe to take out fevers, chills, the "pewter," and so on. (In Appalachia, the Devil was often said to have one pewter eye, and a person who can give the evil eye is said to be "looking for the Devil.") The egg is then broken into a glass of water and read for any signs of the cause of illness. Blood in the yolk means a curse; an eye will form for the evil eye; and the water will become murky for illness (murkiness measures the seriousness of the illness). However, don't be stupid and not go to the doctor if you need to. As I write this, the flu is horrible right now in America and several people have already died because of it. Be as wise as you want, but don't be a fool.

Other rites of transference use trees. To be rid of the chills and "fits," go to an aspen tree and wrap your arms around it. At the place where your fingers meet, carve a hole into the tree with a pocketknife. Back in the day it had to be a stolen pocketknife, but I've used just any one. The hole is then loaded with three hairs taken from the crown of the head and a glob of honey or butter. While doing this, say the following:

> *Aspen tree, aspen tree, I pray to thee,*
> *may you shiver and quake instead of me.*
> *In the name of the Father, the Son, and the Holy Spirit.*
> *Amen.*

The hole is then plugged up with the wood that was removed to transfer the chills to the tree.

Another rite that utilizes a tree is for when you have a toothache. The gums around the tooth are stirred with a toothpick or needle to bring the blood. The blood is then wiped on a strip of white fabric one inch wide by seven inches long. Then find a tree where a root is exposed, ideally about one to two inches in diameter. Once you've found your root, dig down enough so you can wrap the fabric around the root, tie it in a knot, and leave without looking back. This will cure the aching.

Another form of transference is shown in the act of "buying" diseases or the clients themselves, such as someone giving you money and then rubbing your warts for a bit afterward, or buying you from a relative. This confuses the disease spirit because it's not clear who has possession of the ailment or the client themselves, leaving it only one option: to leave.

One's own temperament while doing something can also transfer to things to affect them a certain way. One trick I'm sure most of my local readership has heard of growing up is to be mad as hell when planting any type of pepper. This itself varies by family and location in Appalachia. I personally grew up hearing that you had to piss someone off and then get them to plant a pepper without them knowing about the charm. Hard to do that when everyone knows this, so I'm sure you can just muster up enough anger to plant your own. Bring up things from the past in your head that made you mad. It's probably not psychologically healthy to do so, but you'll have some good peppers come harvest, so screw it!

Transference rites don't focus solely on healing and removing disease, either. They can be done to remove spirits and conjure tricks placed on you. To remove the spirit of a haint from their old home, get a potato and an item that belonged to them in life. Cut the potato in half and hollow out both sides just enough to fit the item inside. Then close the potato up with string. Take this charm to their grave and bury the potato at the heart of it. The spirit will then be transferred and bound to the grave.

To remove a conjuring placed on you, take one hair from the crown of your head, an eyebrow hair, and a nail clipping from your left hand. Bundle these into a bag and blow into it nine times. Take this bundle and leave it at a crossroads far from your home, one that you rarely pass by; the ninth person to pass that crossroads will receive the trick. It is apparent this trick was likely formulated by laypeople and not a conjure person. The laypeople simply took it into their hands with what they knew and transferred the charm to someone else.

Another example of transference is one I believe everyone has heard: eat a lot of carrots so your eyesight and hearing will be good like that of the rabbit. This one is odd, because it doesn't bring the rabbit into direct relation. Instead the only connection is the belief that the rabbit's food, the carrot, is the reason they see and hear so well. Therefore, by eating the rabbit's food, you can also gain those qualities of the rabbit through "implied transference."

Many other transference rites, however, bring the animal into direct relation, such as swallowing a fish's bladder to become a good swimmer, or eating a turtle's heart to become brave.

Lastly, the widespread phenomenon of transference rites appears not in formulas or cures, but in the transition of knowledge from one person to the next. Oftentimes, certain formulas or "gifts," such as fire talking, were only shared with the closest relative of the opposite sex at death. Other times, charms could be shared with only three people, after which point the bearer would lose the gift. And in still other regions, a person could be of any sex and their gift could be shared as much as possible—but those related by blood could not be taught. Since we see here how transference affects the body and is likewise channeled by the body (in the example of planting peppers, mentioned above), let's move on to rites of the body.

BODY RITES

There are several old formulas, stories, and superstitions focusing on parts of the body. In this section, we'll focus primarily on restoring health by treating two crucial parts: the head and the feet.

One of the most widespread is that of keeping the head covered in graveyards; to do otherwise could leave you vulnerable to haints hopping on your back and following you home. The head is also the crown of your soul, the eyes are the windows to it, and the chest is its seat. The head acts like the roof of that home.

The head is the crown of the soul and should be protected. Many people hold superstitious beliefs about hats and other head coverings. It's bad luck to lay a hat on a table or bed. When a black cat crosses a man's path, he's supposed to turn his hat backward until he gets to where he's going in order to avert the foretold bad luck.

For fever, I will make up some redbud tea (from the bark of the tree), and take a very small sip from a straw and blow it on the crown of the sick person's head before they drink the remainder of the tea. Depending on the person and their specific condition, I mix it up with certain prayers and methods that I won't share here. (A good doctor never reveals everything.)

Growing up, whenever we had an earache, my mother would blow tobacco smoke in our ears.

If you ever get a toothache, try holding tobacco smoke in your mouth.

For any pain from the jaw up (fever, toothache, earache, and so on), hold a button made of bone in your mouth until the pain subsides. This cure is somewhat reminiscent of taking the host at church and could very well be a folk invention based on that rite.

Many times, such remedies are bags or curios hung around the neck, like the case with hanging mole feet around the neck of a teething child or wearing a bag of buttercups around the neck for insomnia, confusion, and other maladies of the head.

The feet are the second most vulnerable point of the body: they are the "foundation." One's feet are especially susceptible to being "poisoned" by conjurings and roots placed for the person in the form of powders, dirts, sprinkled water, or buried charms. Sicknesses can also enter through the feet and likewise be drawn out. My grandmother always fussed at me when I was little and my feet were dirty from playing out in the woods barefoot. She'd say, "You best clean them feet or they'll have you walking wrong." Not sure if she was alluding to the whipping I'd get if I didn't clean them or to picking up some sickness, but I didn't leave a lick of dirt on them lest I was to find out!

The head and the feet comprise the top and bottom of the "house" of the soul. The Cherokee believed that the soul lives in the chest, home of the heart and the place we experience half of our existence (the other half being in the mind). In the Freewill Baptist Church, folks are anointed on the forehead, chest, and feet. On the Thursday before Easter, properly known as Maundy Thursday, Baptists wash each other's feet as Jesus washed the feet of others in the Bible. This is to remind them of compassion and humility, but can also offer protection and health to those washed during the Holy Week. Oftentimes, members of the congregation burst into tears, or yell and holler in the presence of the Holy Spirit; other times they simply cry and lay blessings on the one washing them.

The church also anoints from the head to the toes, as shown in Leviticus 14:14–28:

> *14 And the priest shall take some of the blood of the trespass offering, and the priest shall put it upon the tip of the right ear of him that is to be cleansed, and upon the thumb of his right hand, and upon the great toe of his right foot. (Leviticus 14:14)*

The clothes worn on the body also hold special significance in folk magic. You've seen previously how hair is taken from the crown of the head in some formulas to affect initiate change in an ailment, but the feet are also just as useful. Foot track works and shoe magic have appeared in Appalachia in numerous tales and superstitions. If you walk behind someone in their footsteps, it's said they'll die. Placing prayer notes and dried herbs such as red pepper in the shoes is also done in certain formulas for protection from conjuring, to guard against haints, and to attract good fortune.

Old shoes hold the shape of the wearer's foot, and in this way they hold that person's essence. Old shoes were dusted with baby powder, salt, red pepper, and other things at hand for protection from conjure, illness, and accident. Sprinkle "new" salt (a container or packet of salt that has never been opened) in the shoes for good fortune and success. Or take a piece of brown paper bag and fold into it salt, red pepper, and dirt from a church, and place this in your left shoe to prevent yourself being conjured or "shot" at.

Likewise, old preachers may anoint the inner rim of their hat with blessed oil when doing a funeral to keep haints away. Other formulas prescribed burying the unwashed undergarments of someone to make them go mad, lose their hair, or waste away to death. The garments must have been worn so that they contain essential connections to the person through sweat or odor.

The head and feet hold great importance in the magic of Appalachia, especially in cleansing, blessing, and protecting. Around here, you'll go to great lengths to make sure you are upheld, kept clean, and cared for "from the top of your head to the soles of your feet," as the old church prayer goes.

MEASURING RITES

Measuring practices can be seen in a plethora of tales of the Upland South for remedying ailments such as back pain, rheumatism, worms, and inflammation. Silk thread is often used for measuring rites for infants and children, whereas regular yarn, thread, or twine is used for adults in measuring practices.

One practice involves measuring an afflicted or symbolic part of the body with a length of yarn or twine and tying it with a series of knots. Different formulas specify what to do with the knotted yarn. For chills, I will measure the diameter of a person's torso, because that's where the body "shakes and shivers." Use a length of red string to measure and take it out to a tree in the woods. I tie a knot in the line for each day the chills have been present. I then tie the yarn around the trunk and leave it there without looking back. The chills will go to the tree within the same number of days as there are knots in the line.

To remove a fever, measure the girth of the patient's head with white thread. (The color of the string is based on the need of the person or case at hand. The red string for the chills brings the warmth of the blood and sun; a white string is the color of snow to "cool" the fever.) The head is measured because a fever is thought to sit in the head, and it's the first place mothers always feel to check for one. Tie three knots in the thread in the name of the Trinity and place it in a bowl of cold water beneath the bed. The fever usually breaks within the hour.

For someone who has frequent nose bleeds, measure their left ring finger with a white string. The left ring finger is measured because it is "closest to the heart," having a larger artery than on the right hand. Wet the string with the blood from a nosebleed. Then knot the string three times in the name of the Father, the Son, and the Holy Ghost. Take that knotted and bloody thing out to a willow tree and bury it under the dirt, right at the base against the roots, on the east side of the tree. I ain't had a nosebleed since this rite was done for me. That's going on about twelve years now.

Measuring rites don't focus solely on healing. To keep a dog or cat from running away, measure the length of its tail or the length from its left hind foot to the tip of the tail with a holly branch or red string and bury this under the doorstep, including a carefully acquired snip of fur from the scruff of the animal's neck and the tip of their tail.

To "tie a man's nature up," meaning he will only be sexually attracted to you and he won't be running around on you with someone else, measure the length of his penis with a red string. How you go about doing this is your own business. Braid this string with two strips of his dirty underwear and take it to a living honeysuckle bush. Tie the vines around the braid snug, but don't break them. As the vines grow more around it, as they gain bark and strength during the growing season, he'll be closer to you and it'll be harder for him to leave you for another.

Now if a man wants to tie a woman's nature up, he doesn't utilize the measurement of her genitals. Instead, he takes the measurement of her left big toe, her left foot, or her left leg. (Ask any man in Appalachia—our women are always on the go, doing something or another, which may explain the use of the foot and leg here. We also know why the man's genitals are used. Think on it if you need to.) He'll take this measurement of string and urinate on it. The use of urine in American folk magic in very common, and more often than not it is the first relief of the morning that is put to use. When the string is wet with his water, he will bury it under the doorstep, where she'll walk over it. She won't be running around on him again after that. Other ways of tying a partner up involve slugs and genitals, but that's for another book.

Measuring can also be done against an enemy. To cause them grief and struggle, get some soft black dog hair and spin it into yarn with a spindle. Then measure the width of the heel of your enemy's footprint and cut the string to that length. Bore a hole into the western base of a black walnut with a stolen pocketknife and stick the string into the hole with some salt, black pepper, and snakeskin and plug the hole up. Your enemy will be grieving and struggling as long as that's plugged up.

PEGGING, PLUGGING, AND NAILING RITES

Pegging or plugging are the half sisters of measuring in the ways they're employed. Pegging utilizes three parts in its working: first, the measurement of a person or animal compared to a tree; second, the type and age of the tree itself; and third, outgrowing the measurement of the peg.

Pegging rites are usually done with children and their ailments since the main purpose is to outgrow the marking so they likewise outgrow the sickness or problem that was plugged into the hole. Pegging is mostly done with trees, although doorframes, walls, and poles are sometimes used. Nailing is related to pegging solely in the act of holding something or someone down, back, or in place.

To stop up a bleed, place some of the blood into a hole with some honey and plug the hole. Many times peggings that are often done for healing are made into the east side of a tree, or sometimes the hole is made where the sun first hits the tree in the morning, because that's the auspicious direction of the Christian English and pagan natives alike.

You can also plug up your enemy's life or stop up the bladder of the witch who cursed you. One way of doing this is to collect the hair or dirt from the property of the witch who cursed you. Some salt or sugar borrowed from them would work as well. Take this to a pawpaw tree and bore a hole into the wood, at the crotch of the trunk on the western side. Fill the hole with the hair, dirt, or borrowed thing and plug it back up. Then drive three horseshoe nails into the plug. The only way to remove this would be to remove the nails and the plug from the wood and burn the contents.

The pawpaw tree has always been associated with the dead and witchcraft in Appalachia, even before colonization. I call it the Appalachian pomegranate, mountain food for the dead. It has a sweet banana mango flavor to it, but the deer will not eat the fruit and many beasts avoid it also because of the rotting meat smell the flowers give off.

To keep something held down, whether you're wanting your man to stay with you or to remain in the home that you're in, take a wooden peg, stake, or railroad spike and something of the person's out to the west side of your home and drive it down into the ground. Leave a couple inches of the stake above ground. Each day, for seven to nine days, take the stake out and whisper your petition or prayer into the hole. On the final day, drive the stake straight into the ground and cover it up.

DIRECTIONAL RITES

Being that Appalachia has had a crock pot of culture and tradition brewing for a long time, it was bound to occur that certain directions gained sway over the daily activities and secret things of the mountaineer's life. In East Tennessee there's a majority who hold the belief that they descend from the Cherokee. Paired with that belief is the pride placed in the Cherokee's gifts of war, healing, and religion.

The Cherokee people held a noticeable influence in the making of Appalachian folk magic, as our local lore, tales, and cures show. Many cures shared between the two groups in those times are likely to have been pure magic or belief in nature, with no medical theory at their ground.

The Cherokee associated the east with good spirits, the sun, and more. They would address the east in their petitions and prayers to these spirits, especially those for removing witchcraft and disease. They would look to the north, the home of winter or the Blue Man, when healing burns.[1] (The Blue Man was the Cherokee explanation for winter and diseases associated with it.) And they would look to the south for the Red Man for aid with frostbite and other winter-related ailments. Finally, the Cherokee recognized the Black Man or Purple

---

[1] James Mooney, "The Swimmer Manuscript: Cherokee Sacred Formulas and Medicinal Prescriptions," *Bureau of American Ethnology Bulletin* 99 (1932).

Man of the west, who brought death. (The Black Man has many incarnations throughout American folklore, as he is often thought to be the Devil or some dealing spirit who waits at the crossroads. The distinction between the two isn't clear, so they may be the same spirit called upon in witchcraft and death spells.) The duality, significance, and personality of each direction have been partly preserved in lore and tales, some of which were passed down in families like mine.

Today, the formulas that I use from this lore and magic utilize the directions in the same ways. I use the east for healing diseases of the flesh, mending, joining, and charging new things. I use the west to purify and be rid of disease altogether, to send away, to hold down, and for calling rain. I use the south for love, things of physicality, healing diseases of the blood, curing chilblains (inflammation caused by exposure to the cold), good crops, and good fishing. And the north I use for cursing work, keeping things hidden, good root crops (especially those to be sown in the snow), giving disease or "unnatural illness," or curing burns or fevers.[2] Unnatural illness, a changed stomach, or madness are all ways to describe this folk phenomenon, caused by a curse to kill the afflicted. Usually caused by the well-known Goofer Dust, made from powdered grave dirt, spider eggs, and other ugly things laid for the person to walk in, the symptoms were madness, pain, and swelling in the legs to the point of lameness, ending in the afflicted howling like a dog and finally dying.

The Baptist Church we grew up in performed baptisms in the river facing east. We spoke previously about graves being oriented a certain way so the dead face east as well.

When "water witching," some folks start by facing the east and turning counterclockwise. Whichever way the stick first bobs, that's the direction to go in. From the starting place to the area where the sticks dips real good, indicating water, you measure that length; that's

---

[2] David Pickering, Cassell *Dictionary of Superstitions* (Cassell, 1996).

how far you'll dig to reach the water. (Here we see the measuring rites come into play apart from the use of the human body.)

Some cursing formulas recommend taking lichen or wood from the north face of a tree, usually pawpaw or dogwood. Lichen is often powdered and added to food for the work, while formulas that detail taking wood from the north side of the tree only work by splitting the wood open and inserting something like the person's hair or nails before binding the split back together with string.

Through the works of Harry Hyatt, an Anglican minister who collected folklore all over the south and composed it into five volumes, it becomes apparent that the west quarter of one's property was almost always used to keep something or someone where it currently is, be it your employment at work, your man's fidelity, or an enemy.

The directions of up and down also come into play in some ways. When passing a candle over a person, I always move in a downward motion from head to toe. This is done to be rid of something: as the feet are an opening for possible conjure to come in, they are also the exit by which you can remove it. This is applied also to baths. To dispel something, wash downward from head to toe; and to draw something to you, wash upward from the feet to the head.

The clock's hands also created directional use in magic. Move clockwise to go with the sun and grow, or move counterclockwise to go against the sun and diminish. Wounds are rubbed counterclockwise, to undo the harm. The Cherokee used this directional method with snakebite to "uncoil" the serpent, thereby eradicating the poison to effect a cure.

TURNING RITES

Turning rites are a play on directional rites. Mountaineers have used these for generations to undo or prevent things, whether it's bad luck, haints, or disease. It is simple yet effective reversal work, and it is amazing. During a woman's labor, all empty vessels are sometimes turned upside down to prevent the baby from being breech.

An old trick for when you suspect someone's got a candle on you, like they're working roots on you, is to get a small crock or other handle-less pot. On a Wednesday morning, place it in the sink or bathtub upside down under the faucet and let the water slowly drip onto the bottom of the pot until Friday night. That'll put their candle out.

When a black cat crosses your path or you're walking through a graveyard alone, turn your pockets inside out to guard against ill fortune and haints. Some folks turn their hats backward, as mentioned before, or literally turn around three times either clockwise or counterclockwise, depending on the superstition and the location.

There's an old superstition that says if you accidentally put your clothes on inside out then you should leave them that way all day, as it's a sign someone is trying to charm you. Others recommend wearing every garment inside out for nine consecutive days and then taking the clothes to the river to wash them with vinegar to remove any tricks.

Turning also applies to wheels and handles. Take any kind of wheel and turn it backward while reciting Psalm 7:13–17 for nine consecutive days to send conjurings back to their sender, reverse your back luck, and let your enemies catch themselves in the spikes of the wheel:

> *He also prepares for Himself instruments of death;*
> *He makes His arrows into fiery shafts.*
> *Behold, the wicked brings forth iniquity;*
> *Yes, he conceives trouble and brings forth falsehood.*
> *He made a pit and dug it out,*
> *And has fallen into the ditch which he made.*
> *His trouble shall return upon his own head,*
> *And his violent dealing shall come down on his own crown.*
> *I will praise the* Lord *according to His righteousness,*
> *And will sing praise to the name of the* Lord *Most High.*

An owl hooting near the house is said to be a death omen. One old remedy calls for every person of the family to take their shoes and place them under a bed upside down to deter death from visiting the home.

To protect against being conjured by any roots you may walk over, take a pocketknife and cut the soles out of your shoes. Flip them over and put them in the other shoe (that is, place the upside-down left sole into the right shoe and vice versa).

When there's a bothersome haint haunting the home, we will take up some old horseshoes in red fabric. We then hang them above each doorframe, pointing downward. In Appalachia this is a symbol of the home: to keep luck in, keep the points turned up; to get rid of evil spirits, put the points down. Oddly enough, the way to guard against conjuration entails the points be turned upward, but the horseshoe be wrapped in "silver paper" or tinfoil.

Other formulas describe the turning or flipping of portraits for various reasons. My family will turn the photo of a family member upside down to call them home for any reason. To return a lover, get a photograph of them, a bowl of salt, and a glass of water. Set the water between you and the bowl of salt and take their photo and turn it upside down and flip it away from you. The photo should be facedown with the head toward you. Cover it with the salt. Then dip your fingers in the water and sprinkle them over the salt while telling them to think about you, to want you, and to yearn to see you. Pray for them to need you as though they were thirsting for water because of all the salt.

If someone hasn't been so kind to you, take their photo and wrap it facedown around a pokeberry root, which is known to be poisonous. Take this bundle and bury it where they'll walk across it. Once the photo fades away, so will their health. Alternatively, wrap a white handkerchief around the framed picture and hang it on a wall by driving a knife through it with the photo facing the wall.

If you just want to jinx them a bit, a run of bad luck, basically, turn their photo upside down into a bowl of brown rice and leave it in a dry place. This will dry up their luck. Take it out and put it upright again to put their luck back.

QUINCUNX RITES

Quincunx is a particular pattern that is abundant in all American folk magic practices. A Quincunx consists of four points or corners with a central mark, recalling the symbol of the cross and the crossroads. In many folk traditions, American and foreign, the crossroads is a meeting place between worlds, between man and the spirits. It's home to the Black Man, to lost souls who wander about, and to the dead in general. The cross symbolizes protection, sacrifice, and revelation. Many things are worked at the crossroads, and likewise anything done is left there for the spirits to continue the work.

New salt is often used by the workers of Appalachia. One such trick is done to give someone bad luck: make a simple cross or X on the ground where they'll walk over it. X's pair into this same symbolism and are a common symbol used in Appalachian folk magic. To protect children from the evil eye, a red X was embroidered into the left-leg hem of their underwear. In the Baptist Church, the brow is anointed with the cross. And, as we've seen, the crossroads symbol is invoked by placing four tiles around a crop field, with one more placed in the center.

Crosses and X's are used in rites of cleansing and cursing; sending out and drawing in since they lead in every direction going out or in. I have an old knife-tool that my father found and gave to me. On the one side of the handle there are three marks (X X X) carved into the wood. The number three here likely connects to the Holy Trinity. X's are also used to cancel out illnesses, followed by the cross to bless after the cleanse.

If a woman wanted to keep her man at home so he wouldn't leave her, she'd go to a dirt crossroads and make a cross in the dirt. From the center of the mark she'd take some dirt and pair it with his hair, which she would then wrap in brown paper and bury at the door of the home.

SIDE RITES

You will notice throughout this book that many workings and remedies specify doing something on the left or right side. Irish lore is filled with formulas that prescribed things to a certain side. One still acknowledged today is to carry an iron nail in the left hand or left pocket to protect from being conjured by the little people.

The left hind foot of the rabbit is carried because the left side is traditionally associated with luck, and the alluring hind legs allow the rabbit to escape from predators (although it doesn't seem to have been lucky for the rabbit in the end). While we're on the topic of rabbits, their feet are sometimes carried by livestock or people to protect them from the evil eye because rabbits are born with their eyes already open. I've also been told that the foot gets stronger the longer it is carried and the more dried out it gets.

In Appalachian formulas, the left side is symbolic of warding, protection, and getting rid of something, such as tossing spilt salt over your left shoulder to "blind the Devil." The right side is another story altogether. Jacks or sachets are prescribed by folklore to be carried in the right pocket. The charms carried on the right side are those that affect an influence, they administer the will in some way; so a jack to get a new job or convince someone to do a favor for you would be carried on the right side. The left side deflects and gently brings, while the right side enacts and gives influence; this influence can also be to repel or draw, but mostly when the work is to affect others in some way. To protect from conjure, items can be carried on either side, really, so place red pepper, black pepper, and salt wrapped in newspaper in both shoes to do the job. For a healing charm, that should be carried on the left in some manner—in the shoe, in a pocket, or pinned to the inner hem of your clothes. To bring a lover back, roots would be thrown over the right shoulder. However, formulas detailing use of the right side have become extremely rare to come across—either documented or by word of mouth.

In regards to the rabbit's foot again (it's one of my favorite charms, if you couldn't tell), I prefer to use the right hind feet for safeguarding against harm, curing hiccups, and keeping off conjuring. The left side seems to have become the universal way to carry it, however. What has been preserved is the reasoning behind both: the left is the more vulnerable side, better for carrying protective and curing works, whereas the right side is the more dominant one, used for drawing in, keeping up, and setting down—but is also likewise employed in works of guarding and protecting.

If you do not hunt rabbits for meat, I would speak to friends and family who do or even go to your local taxidermist. You can get the foot dried or preserve it yourself by burying it in a bucket of salt and baking soda and leaving it for about a month to dry. You can also look online, but folks rarely specify left or right foot and may not even know how to tell. The ones for sale are often the front foot.

7

SAINTS ON THE RIVER
Spirits of Southern Appalachia

Theres a bit more to spirit lore than all the ghost stories. There are real spirits in these hills whose voices are heard from the grave-yards and pews, and whose apparitions are multiple: from white bags of cotton tied to a bridge to floating lights wandering the forests late at night. There are spirits that are good and helpful; spirits that frighten us with warnings; and still others yonder, the ones that come for you and everything you got, sent by another or the Devil himself.

We test those malignant spirits by our faith, and we discern their intentions by the way our hair stands on end and the way our gut tells us to react. Many of the southern doctors of these hills conversed with and received aid from unseen friends. As a people who have been isolated in these dark hills, we've learned the noises that go bump in the night and the difference between real voices and those traversing worlds, nameless or not.

The ghosts of folkloric witches and conjurors peer through local stories and memories, hiding behind the hills and cliffs of Appalachia; the good neighbors, spirits who continue their shenanigans when the church bells aren't ringing. There are stories of giant bees, huge magic snakes that lurk beneath pools of water, and an unseen giant hunter named Tsul'Kalu, literally meaning "slanting eyes," who stalks the cliffs of the Blue Ridge Mountains. Some of these we will meet here.

The granny witches primarily worked with God, as did the doctors of the Cherokee, Delaware, and Choctaw. God is always called upon in the most tender way in prayers for healing, often called "Papa," or "Daddy," as my Aunt Marie called Him. God is a protector. He brings justice and comfort, and "the God on the mountain is the same in the valley," to quote an old hymn. He is thought of as the first conjuror, creating the world in six days. The beliefs and stories of these spirit folk are as varied in creed and belief as the folks who tell about them. We apply Scripture in the works here: we test to see if they are of God. Whether good folk, angels, saints, or ghosts, most of us belief they just *are*, as everything else in creation is under God.

By historical and oral accounts, only a handful of these spirits have been recorded and identified in the practice of the Appalachian doctor. Many times no singular spirit is spoken to, but instead a multitude is addressed. Spiritual occurrences during this work have also been recorded, from foggy morning mists taking the shape of unseen guests to invisible presences toking on a lit tobacco pipe. Likewise, patterns occur throughout these tales, especially with the class of spirits we call haints. These varied spirits are called many names such as spooks, hoodoos, boogers, mares, and angels.

Growing up, Nana spoke often of angels flying over when your hair stood on end, and said that a tree grows in the space where angels have trod. She spoke of "elves" who stole things and replaced them in the oddest places. When we dream of passed loved ones, we know they are truly visits. But if we dream of a birth or of someone being dead, it's an omen of death. There's a lot of trust placed in the unseen guests who come in the name of God to help or warn. We will meet some of them here. But first we need to know how to speak to them.

DREAMS

To dream of the dead isn't always a good thing, let alone if the person you see is currently alive. The mountaineers have held an age-old belief that spirits can come to us in dreams and that God gives some folks a special gift for dreaming this way. This is what we call "dreaming true" or "dreaming right" even though the contents of the prophetic inner play may be daunting. My mother and grandmothers have always been visited by spirits or saw future events in their dreams, and this gift is closely related to the sight.

Every time my mother has a bad dream, she'll wait until after breakfast before calling me. She's bound to the old saying that any dream spoken of before breakfast will come true. We don't chance it, especially with bad dreams. This gift is held by many people, including those outside Appalachia, but it cannot be controlled at will.

I have only dreamed true a couple times. I've tried everything from meditation to lucid dreaming to try to dream true at will, to just peer beyond a little bit, until I realized it's not by my hand but by that of the spirits who bring the message. It's very hard to tell the difference between regular dreams and those that are visions of future events. Generally, the messages of dreaming true will be remembered, while other times the dreamer is left only with a feeling that something ain't right.

There are a few common beliefs in Appalachia about your dreams held by normal folk. To dream of a birth or wedding is a sign of a death; likewise, a dream of a death is a sign of birth. To see a living person dead entails a death omen above their head. If you see someone who has already passed, they may be giving you a sign of how they are: if they're running around aimlessly, either their spirit is not at peace or they are in "hell," according to Nana; but to see them calm, they are at peace.

Pay attention to your dreams. Dreaming true isn't composed of symbolic meanings; what happens in the dream will happen in real life. So if a diseased relative tells you that Johnny is in danger, then he *is* in danger. Dreams are straightforward messages from God and the spirits. Symbolic dreams don't necessarily give specifics like that, but a "true dream" can be embedded in a regular dream. It takes years of heeding them to be able to tell the difference. However, aside from dreams, spirits can make their presence known in the most mundane of ways.

SIGNS FROM THE SPIRIT WORLD

A few weeks after my Papaw Trivett passed away, we began to find small white feathers everywhere. In the strangest places they would be found, or they'd simply float down out of nowhere. We'd find feathers in the food cabinets, in pots stored under the stove, in the fridge, or we'd all be sitting in the living room and they'd fall down from the ceiling. We spent weeks trying to find where they were coming from. Only problem was, we didn't own anything stuffed with feathers. Never did and never have.

The feathers were often paired with the smell of Papaw's Old Spice cologne. On my grandparents' anniversary, my grandmother was heading to the store and found pennies laid out in a line going from the front door of the house to the driver's side of her car. She still has those pennies today.

Papaw always fixed dinner on Thanksgiving, and we looked especially forward to his famous chicken and dumplings. On the first Thanksgiving after his death, we decided to just eat out because those memories were too hard on us; he'd had his seventh heart attack on the day after the holiday that year. When we decided to eat out, the cabinet doors in the kitchen continuously opened and slammed shut for days afterward. He must've been mad that no one made his dumplings and the family didn't all congregate at the table. So we decided to cook the following year. As we were all sitting around the small, wood leaf table in the kitchen, we noticed that a luna moth had landed on the outer screen of the back door. "I'm glad you could make it, Daddy," Mama said.

The luna moth is a fascinating creature of the Appalachian hills. Growing up, we were taught to never disturb them or catch them or it would bring bad luck, because they carry souls of the dead and messages from the other side. During their life span they go through a handful of stages before reaching adulthood. When they become adults and emerge from their wraps a changed creature, they no longer have mouths! You read that right. In the last days of their life, they no longer partake of the food of the living. The mountaineers would have had no knowledge of this, nor of the occult symbolism offered in this biological fact. Their last sole purpose during this stage is to reproduce. The mountaineers simply held to old tradition that they were associated with the ghosts of the dead. That fact, in itself, is amazing to me.

Dogs also play an important role in Appalachian folklore. Strange dogs bring messages from the dead, mostly in regards to danger or ill coming to the home. Whether it is a sighting of a black dog with red eyes that's come to warn of death, known as Black Shuck, or a simple white ghost dog that sits and waits in the front yard. Nothing will scare it away because it will not leave until its owner, Death, visits the home.

This same meaning is applied to many other animals, particularly those that are white or albino. White doves are a message of death. And if you've lived in these mountains all your life, then I presume you've heard of the "witching deer." In both the Irish and Cherokee mythos, white or black animals are often thought to be witches or some creature from another world. This belief still persists today, and we've had countless people who wouldn't step foot in our home because of the black cats we had. The belief these animals were witches may have been the reason their furs, bones, or guts were used for various purposes, such as the rabbit's foot for good luck or the black cat's blood for healing rashes.

Other signs from the spirit world include sounds. You'll often hear bells ringing far off when angels or little folk are present. Haints and bad spirits make their presence known by breaking and throwing things or whispering in one's ear. Hearing babies cry that aren't there, either in the house or out in a graveyard, is also a sign of wayward souls.

The materialized form these lost souls often take is that of glowing lights floating about the graveyards and woods at night. The most famous of these lights, called jack-o'-lanterns or will-o'-the-wisps, walk about the hillsides and lead travelers and other folks astray down into the rivers or lakes to be drowned. These strange lights were explained as lost souls, beginning with the old tale of Jack.

Jack was a mean old drunkard who kept having run-ins with the Devil come to take his soul to hell. Each time, Jack outwitted the Devil and bought himself more time. After a while, the Devil got tired of it all and moved on. When Jack finally died, he was locked out of heaven for his drunken deeds, so he took the road down to hell. But alas, not even the Devil wanted him anymore, and so Jack couldn't get in. He was left to wander the earth alone forever. But the Devil felt sorry for Jack, so he tossed him a hot coal from hell to light his way. Jack hollowed out a gourd and placed the hot coal inside, and thus the jack-o'-lantern was born.

The Cherokee were especially afraid of these "fire carriers" and dared not go near them or try to investigate. Folk belief tells of fire carriers bringing madness and rage to those who see them. I have never dared call these up, and neither should you. Lord knows what would answer on the other end of the line.

PROTECTION FROM HAINTS

The word *haint* applies to a multitude of different spirits with varying dispositions, including "demons," lost souls, and ghosts, plus Yunwi Tsunsdi' (*yun-wee joon-stee*), or Cherokee little people. It is basically a southern corruption of *haunt*. Many devices and taboos were developed against their intrusion into our homes, dreams, and lives in a negative way.

Iron has historically been a universal method of protecting against a massive number of things, from disease and evil spirits to bad tempers and the evil eye. Because of this, many charms and tricks have developed on either side of the pond into modern times. To keep one's livestock from being shot by the magic of the little folk or witches, you would use slack water, which is the water used by a blacksmith to cool the iron. Add this water to the waterholes or buckets the animals drink out of, or pour it out over their backs while saying the Lord's Prayer. To avert the evil eye or any other enchantments being placed on a newborn, a 9-inch nail was driven into one of the posts or legs of the crib. Local lore prescribes you to touch something made of iron after someone compliments you or you suspect ill intent in their words.

As I mentioned previously, a horseshoe wrapped in tinfoil and hung on the door will keep away conjurings, witches, and haints. Another remedy for haunting with the horseshoe was to place it in the fireplace and throw a handful of salt over it. As long as the horseshoe remains warm, no evil can enter the home.

Charms that may be carried to guard against haints and evil spirits include a bag of new salt hung around the neck; an iron nail in the pocket; a toby containing mistletoe, tobacco, and lichen or moss from the east side of an oak tree; and a rabbit's foot. You could even just keep your pockets turned inside out.

To keep the dead out of your dreams, hang coral on the bedpost. Some old-timers in Tennessee, Virginia, North Carolina, and others recommend tossing a few handfuls of salt and mustard seed on the doorstep at night based on the premise that haints and evil spirits cannot enter until they've counted each grain and every seed, by which time the sun will be up and it'll be too late for them to pester you.

The scattering and counting belief is rampant through Europe and the Americas. Other forms of this are to keep a Bible by the front door so the spirits will have to count every letter on every page, or hang a sieve on the outside of the door so they'll have to count every hole in the mesh. May seem a bit wacky to have a kitchen utensil hung there, but really, who isn't strange in these hills?

SEEING AND INTERACTING WITH SPIRITS

In Appalachia there are multiple methods for seeing and conversing with spirits. We covered the communication via dreams at the start of this chapter, separated because it occurs in the dream state and is often involuntary. The dead show up in dreams to *bring* us messages, in contrast to us calling out to them for assistance. But spirits regularly interact with us in our daily lives, often without our knowledge, except in extreme circumstances.

There have been many occasions when my mother or me have had close calls while driving because we've seen in the rearview mirror my papaw sitting in the backseat. Other times, my grandmother will be sitting in her recliner at home and Papaw will rock it from the back like he used to, to get her attention.

Other tales are told of speaking with spirits through knocking on tables to get their attention, which seems to be common among root workers everywhere in the South who knock on the ancestor table when leaving offerings or calling out for help.

Those with the sight are best able to communicate with spirits. Sight is separate from regular psychic abilities and exclusively given by God at birth. It's said to be given to a child born blue or with a caul over their eyes, although some regions of Appalachia hold a superstition that being born via C-section or at night—and specifically at midnight—can enable you to see spirits as well. This enables the person to see and speak with spirits as well as foretell the future or just know things with no explanation. However, not every person born in one of these circumstances shows the ability, nor can it just be claimed.

In Appalachia we have a few unspoken laws: never lie, never steal, and never cheat. It is simply taboo, and anyone known to do these things will, from then on, be seen as flawed in character. When it comes to these gifts, I've never heard of one person ever claiming they had it. It was always said of them by other people, or the person would keep their humility, saying, "I don't know why folks insist it's me who does it when it's just the Lord." To those with a gift, they were simply following God and doing His will. The person's sight was further proven through their tried-and-true reputation of predictions and dreams given to them through the gift either for themselves or others.

Most folks in Appalachia simply pray to the dead in mourning or during adversities. We sometimes think God's heard enough from us, so we will occasionally turn to the dead first with our pleas. There's been many a time I've heard Mama pray, "Daddy, help me with this." Some people, however, just can't get past the dead being gone, which is reflected in some charms and recommendations for someone without the gift to be able to see or speak with spirits.

The first I ever heard of was to wipe the slick from the corner of a dog's eye with your finger and rub it on your own eyes. Another one says to eat a tablespoon of salt every morning for nine mornings upon waking. Don't speak to anyone, or speak at all until the salt is consumed (without drink). (This seems nearly impossible to do.) The last method is to go to the site of a grave on the ninth day after burial and it's said you'll be able to speak with and see the deceased.

Many old healers from back in the day are said to have done something to please the good neighbors so much they were gifted with particular knowledge, whether through a chance meeting or from falling asleep under a hawthorn, which is still said to make folks go mad. Others are said to have walked backward three times around a graveyard while saying the Lord's Prayer and afterward they just *knew* what to do.

The crossroads is also an important place for spirit work in Appalachia. Not only does it symbolize the cross, but it also brings together the corners of the earth. Cross-streams are sometimes used as well; the place where two creeks meet and become one is said to be a location of powerful healing. Crossroads are used in opening the path to remove obstacles, or close someone's roads so they can't get away with something, like a criminal or thief. The crossroads represent coming and going, movement and deadlock, and communication between us and the spirits, in that in-between space where the living and the dead speak.

Aside from places such as crossroads or graveyards, there are also particular times that are best for speaking to spirits, such as the hour of midnight. My family holds fast the belief in the ghost hour of 3:00 a.m., when you're most likely to wake up startled to "nothing."

Other times aren't based on the clock at all but by natural phenomenon, such as when the clouds roll down the mountain or the fog hangs low and dense, and the spirits "rise down" the hills. There's a special spirit to the fog here in East Tennessee. She seems to rise and blanket the land in mystery. It's said if you peer into it long enough, you'd see the dead walking around: civil war soldiers, slaves, handmaidens, farmers, Cherokee mothers. Shadows of a people gone but not. A memory of a time that was and still is . . . somewhere.

This I have experienced firsthand in only two cases. The first was driving to the gas station on a foggy morning at 3:00 a.m. As I was passing by the churchyard down the road, I saw what I thought were two people walking. Upon getting closer, a streetlight revealed that all that was there were two foggy pillars of smoke. As I continued on by, they dispersed. The second one occurred right after midnight and it was real foggy. I was driving through the hills (between Kingsport and

Boone's Creek, for you locals), and I saw a woman walking on the side of the road, clear as day, dressed in old-fashioned attire that consisted of a deep red blouse and a long, gauzy white skirt, complete with glasses that sat on the bridge of her nose. As I drove by, she turned and looked at me through her spectacles and the glare from the headlights reflected back at me. After passing, I could see no one in the car mirrors.

Remember Miz Wilson? Folks say she'd chant and whisper, entertaining the dead and other spirits in the rocks and riverbanks; she'd chant and charm all night. Come daybreak, Ol' Miz Wilson would retire to her shack and the spirits would return to their place in the rocks. Folks would see her come out, right early in the morning when the sun had just risen and the mists and fog were rising from the water's surface. She'd get her a round stone and twirl it in her hands, rubbing her thumbs around and around on it, while whispering and gazing into the fog, seemingly hypnotized by it. Folks say she was talking to the dead, the little folk, or the Devil himself. While no one knows for sure whom Ol' Miz Wilson was talking to, I figure it had to be an interesting conversation, don't you think? This technique seems to be a preoccupation of the thumbs and fingers rubbing over the stone, perhaps to subdue and distract the "right mind" for spiritual communication. I've tried my hand at it before and have my stone still, and as far as I can gather, it helps ease you into another space.

WORKING WITH THE DEAD

Working with the dead is one of the most popular yet least understood practices in folk magic. Many people read about it online and just hop down to the graveyard for some dirt, but it isn't that simple. Spirits don't just make miracles on request. They'll do favors and offer services in exchange for something—usually pennies or other coins, jars of moonshine, cigarettes, food, or perfume left on the grave. When I am buying dirt from a grave, I will simply tell the spirit, "I ain't stealing nothing, cause I'm leaving this here in its place," or "I'm buying some of your dirt here for such and such reason for such and such offering."

Graveyards are the focus of all kinds of weird tales, and they have become a place of importance in the making of many formulas for protection, luck, love, healing, and cursing. Some recipes call for dirt from the grave of a police officer or a doctor for varied reasons. Then people go out and get it with no question. But the problem here is that you are employing the aid of a spirit you know nothing about. What if the doctor in life abused his patients or the police officer was crooked? Not everything can be found in a Google search or a book. Not even here. Usually folks were buried in a family hilltop cemetery, so family stories have information about who did what as a profession—whether they were a miner, a shoemaker, a sheriff, a doctor. Folks knew everybody in town back then as well. It's not like this anymore, so you need to be careful of who you approach in the graveyard.

The dead aren't all kind, and there are more secrets in each grave than you'll ever know. We work with the dead to have them complete a task on our or someone's behalf and will use the dirt from the grave in the tricks to bring their power into the work. When you go to a graveyard to employ a spirit or buy dirt, I encourage you to use the previously mentioned ways of protecting yourself from haints. Other precautions I take at a graveyard include the following: Never step over a grave, as it will bring misfortune. Don't point at a grave, or you'll be stricken with illness. Come alone and leave alone, and as you leave do not look behind you until you pass the first crossroads home, or you'll be vulnerable to a spirit hopping on your back. I won't even look in the rearview mirrors of the car until I pass the first crossroads. You can avoid this vulnerability by wearing a hat of some kind; most folks always wore a hat or bonnet to funerals and grave decorations anyway.

If you're still wondering about being stricken with illness, it does happen. Half of the time, weird illnesses can be caused unconsciously from the lingering ghosts of relatives pining for their family, and it will especially affect a person they were particularly close to. Other times, it can be a conscious act on the part of the spirit. But believe me, if you piss off the dead, bringing sickness is barely the bottom of the bag of tricks they have in store.

Before doing any work with a spirit you have no prior experience with, in life or death, it is always best to test the spirits to "see if they are of God," or that they mean well and can be trusted. Remember that even the Devil can recite Scripture. Always trust your gut. Say a prayer asking God to give you the spiritual power of discernment to see if the spirits mean well. Uneasy feelings like knots in the pit of your stomach, gusts of warm air, chills, and wind blowing from the north are signs you need to hightail it out of there.

Now that's not to say we never work with bad haints. It's just not recommended for those who aren't trained to do so, as the spirits of thieves and criminals can go rogue. Some of the above signs can be results of fear, but you don't need that here. My Mamaw Hopson always said, "fear is just faith backward." It means you're looking in the wrong direction instead of trusting the Creator and your ancestors. I don't believe wiser words have ever been spoken in these hills. Some of the old formulas recommended gathering dirt from the graves of certain people, mostly based on profession, habit, and cause of death: a man who was a drunkard, a sinner, an unbaptized child, and someone who died badly are the most frequent targets. But for now, I recommend you stick with the folks you knew in life.

When entering a graveyard or cemetery, there's a widespread tradition of giving an offering to the guardian spirit of the cemetery in order to enter and be under their protection. There are two beliefs about this guardian spirit. The first originates from the African traditions. They believe that the guardian spirit is the first person laid to rest in the graveyard and is charged with the duty of keeping watch over it forever. In Scotland and Ireland, they believe it's the last person to be buried who is charged with keeping watch from sunset to sunrise every day. This guardian is discharged only when the next person is buried.[3]

The dead are employed for multiple reasons. Usually, your own beloved departed can manage just about everything you need help with. If you need protection, go to the grave of that person who was an old-fashioned "mama bear" and gather the dirt from the heart of the grave. If you need money, go to the luckiest person you knew. My Papaw Trivett used to go down to Cherokee and gamble a lot. He had a bit of a problem, but it was rare that he lost. He also owned his own contracting business, and he ran a good show at restoring and flipping multiple houses throughout my mama's childhood. If I ever need help or an extra buck, I go to his grave.

LITTLE PEOPLE

Stories from from the Irish, Scottish, and Cherokee continue in Appalachia about little people who live in the caves and treetops, creeks and hills, and even tunnels beneath old colleges. The Cherokee held these beliefs long before the white foot fell on this soil. The little people from Cherokee stories were called Yunwi Tsunsdi'. They were described as being like the Cherokee in attire and language, and somewhat in culture. They are a handsome people and barely knee-high, with long hair to their ankles.

The Cherokee speak about one particular little "wizard" who acts like an Appalachian puck in his hillside activities. (Puck, or *puca*, in folklore is an English trickster spirit.) This malicious trickster dwarf is De'tsata (*day-jah-tah*). His story goes like this: A young Cherokee boy ran off into the forests to avoid getting a whopping from his mother. Ever since, he has remained invisible to avoid the spanking from his

---

[3] Pickering, *Cassell Dictionary of Superstitions*.

mother. Whether he became invisible on his own or he ate the food of the Yunwi Tsunsdi' is up for debate amongst storytellers. (Eating the food of the little people is a universal phenomenon and usually traps the person in their realm. In a similar Cherokee story, a young boy goes to live in the woods and can't return because he has eaten the animal's food, and became the first black bear himself.) They say the invisible boy loves to hunt birds and make a ruckus in the forests. Anytime deer are spooked by something or birds flutter in great numbers from their resting places for no apparent reason, they say it's him chasing them for fun.

The Cherokee hunters would often lose their arrows while hunting, and they blamed it on De'tsata. To find them, the hunter would threaten him with a spanking. The Cherokee believe that De'tsata has been invisible for centuries and in that time he has had multiple children who look just like him and also have his same name.

The little folk aren't very trusting of humans, especially the white man. Cherokee lore tells us they aided lost travelers in the forests, warned the people of impending danger, and helped the conjure or medicine men of the tribe through whispers and dreams. Some stories even tell of layfolk Indians, those not versed in magic or medicine, owning little people and feeding them cornbread or milk in return for protecting their property from theft or vandalism. They also led people to safety and even taught the medicines of a plant in dreams for the sick. They were also the ones who took the human soul to the spirit world.

It takes a lot to gain the trust of the little people and acquire their aid in times of adversity. They don't accept being mocked or gossiped about, and there are many tales of them bringing sickness to those who do so. One story I heard growing up was of a boy walking along a river when he saw a little man sitting on a stone in the middle of the water. The man told the boy not to come any farther, but he persisted and didn't want to be ordered around by a short man such as him. The little boy threw rocks at the man, and each time the rock hit the man it had no effect. He was unharmed. The little man began to laugh and disappeared. The boy went home and told his parents about it all. The father scolded him and told him he needs to go back and apologize before all sorts of bad things befall the family. The boy wouldn't listen. Every night after that, the boy would be found sleepwalking and close to throwing himself out the window. After a few days of this, the father forced the boy to take some food back to the river where the little man was seen. After that, the little folk were appeased and nothing bad befell the family.

The little people of Appalachia are separated in different clans or tribes based on their temperament. The Rock clan is composed of malicious dwarves whose sole task is to lead man to harm or death. The Laurel clan are tricksters, yet rewarding to work with, as their tricks almost always include a bit of humor. The Laurels are to blame for fishing hooks getting caught in rocks and logs at the bottom of lakes and rivers; however, they were also the cause of babies laughing and smiling in their sleep. (Today, this is attributed to angels.) The Dogwood care the most about the human predicament. They are the primary helpers of lost children, the starving, and people in danger on the mountains. The little people, regardless of clan, have been detailed to have white, black, or golden skin like the Cherokee. Sometimes they speak Tsalagi, the language of the Cherokee, but other times they talk in their own native tongue.

To eat the food of a tribe of nature spirits meant that person was now part of that tribe and would never return to or see their kin again. The story of Forever Boy tells this tale. Forever Boy did not want to grow up. All of his human friends talked about what they wanted to do when they became men, how much game they would hunt. Forever Boy didn't want this. He wanted to stay a kid forever and have fun in the creeks. He didn't want the responsibility of a man.

His father told him he needed to learn certain things soon so he would be ready for manhood. His father said he would take him the next day to his uncle and there he would learn everything about being a man. (In Cherokee society it was the closest male relative of the mother who taught her sons about being a man.)

The boy went to the creek and cried his heart out. He didn't want to go to his uncle's house and learn to be a man. He was content with being just a boy. The animals of the forest had gathered around him and were telling him something. "Come back to the creek early tomorrow, in the morning." So he went home.

In the morning, he went back to the creek and the animals were waiting for him. They were telling him something different now: "Look behind you." Forever Boy looked behind him and found all the little people happy to see him. They told him, "You don't have to grow up. Come and live with us and you'll never become a man. You can play with us in the creek forever. We will pray to Creator and He will give your parents a vision that you are safe." The little people gave the boy a root of some kind that was roasted. Some say it was a duck potato (*Sagittaria latifolia*). Legend has it he has remained with the little people and is still a little boy.

Those taken in by the little people either by welcome or by trapping often remain gone from their people for years, although the celebrations and festivities held by the "neighbors," as I call them, only last until dawn. To this day, a lot of people (native or not) will shy away from any strange music or laughter heard in the forests. Many times you wouldn't find the source of the drums or singing anyway, because the direction it comes from will change. Other times, you will find it. Lord have your soul if your intrusion angers them, too.

They are said to have joined in the dances of the tribes, appearing as beautiful young women who enticed the men so much, they didn't notice the goat or deer legs the women had until sunrise when the women would start walking off and disappear with no trace. If you decide to work with these neighbors, never go searching for them. Don't intrude on their space or try to find them. Simply take an offering outside and start talking to them. They'll hear it if they happen to be around. Make a deal with them—continued offerings for a task done on their part—and then lay the offerings down. Never throw their offerings or gifts on the ground, because they aren't animals. I can't stress this enough.

Sometimes, the little people can be petitioned for emergencies or things that are a lost cause. However, if things go wrong, it can't be undone. When you go to them, you are recognizing that whatever charms they perform for you can only be reversed by them. You never want to go to them for love workings. More often than not, it will not be like you hoped, and it is hard to convince them to reverse the charm. The chances of them actually doing this for you are low—even if you offer tobacco, which is traditionally the best offering to anything in these hills.

In the lore of the Old and New World, white animals were believed to be connected to the little people or actually be little people in animal form. This was often paired with the transformational abilities attributed to witches. Other times, white animals were simply believed to be messengers from the dead or angels in heaven. Strangely, the native people of Appalachia hold beliefs parallel with this, especially the white dog. These mixed, and the mountaineer's stories filled with "witchin'" animals such as the albino weasel, snake, deer, bird, or fish. They were attributed with supernatural powers and were honored by tradition as omens of luck, death, and witchcraft. Examples of these are the white dog come to warn about coming death and the witching deer said to be the source of the most powerful madstone, as it was used by natives and colonizers alike.

ANIMAL SPIRITS

This section isn't about animal spirit guides; I'm talking about working with the actual spirits of deceased animals. Appalachian stories are filled with tales about animals that stem from Europe or the native tribes. My father taught me that the black bear was watched to see what plants and berries were good to eat. Stories abound with animals bringing luck or death. Remedies are filled with prescriptions utilizing the feet, eyes, urine, and organs of animals.

Now here's where I need to make a legal statement: Animal abuse, stealing animals, and hunting and fishing out of season are illegal in the United States. Any part or byproduct of migratory birds is illegal to possess in any form, be it eggs, feathers, nest materials, or other things. This is according to the Migratory Bird Treaty Act of 1918. You also need to know about what animal parts you can import or posses in the state you live in, as well as which animals are endangered.

That being said, some remedies and tricks call for crow or robin eggs, salamanders that could be endangered, and the extraction of things from an animal while it is still alive or having it die for a charm. For example, an old cure for whooping cough, seizures, and pneumonia was to catch a rainbow trout on a Sunday and lay the live fish on the chest of the patient, letting it flail about until it dies. As the fish dies, so does the disease or sickness. These types of formulas are many and include such things as suffocating, drowning, gutting, and so on.

I will not speak more on those here; I simply bring it up to remind you that this work was not coined by people who "sought a connection with nature."

Since the purpose of this book is to exhume Appalachian folk magic from its deathbed, I also took into account the current laws regarding the possession and hunting of animals as well as the vulnerability status of all these animals. We live in a different Appalachia today than our elders did. We have to admit that Appalachia has changed and its laws have changed with it. Because of this I promote ethical practices in regards to using animal parts and plants. Do so legally, don't buy things you're not allowed to have in your state, and don't further endanger a species for your own gain.

What I will offer is the bit of lore available in regard to the spirits of animals and how you can work with them. I have a coyote pelt tacked to my living room wall. Surrounding the pelt are chicken feet and flowers. I contracted a deal with the spirit of the coyote to warn me in my dreams of danger and to run off my enemies. I've tenderly named him Ol' Blue. Sometimes, upon returning from somewhere I will scratch the pelt between the ears to show some love.

Now, before I begin a relationship with the spirit of an animal, I always get their consent. Some animals have a huge distaste for humankind due to us destroying their habitats and the abuse they've endured at the hands of man. Some will never be forgiving. This reality is echoed in the Cherokee story of how and why medicine was created: At the start, man and animal had a covenant set between them. The animals would willingly give themselves up in the hunt, giving meat for food, horns for weapons, and fur for warmth, as long as man did the prescribed rituals of prayer and thanksgiving in return for the sacrifice. Man eventually abandoned this practice, hunting deer in large numbers, with no regard given to the beasts and always taking more than was needed. The animals banded together and realized that man can no longer be trusted. Man would no longer acknowledge the covenant between man and beast, so in retaliation the animals decided that for every hide stolen and for every beast killed without gratitude they would send a disease of some kind to the humans to make them suffer and die. In response to this, the plants of the forests and hills spoke and said for every disease the animals placed on man's back, they would offer a medicine to cure him. However, in Cherokee healing, some animals also assisted in healing certain diseases and ailments: the buzzard helped ward off all illnesses, the beaver aided with teething children because of its strong teeth, and the deer helped with frostbite because its hooves are immune to it.[4] The wolf and fox were also called for help with frostbite.

This story is the reason so much care was taken in the hunting and handling of the body after the animal was killed. I do the same with any animal part I acquire. I will pray to their spirit, apologizing for any harm brought to them by man, and I will wash the bones or fur tenderly, trying my best to ease the pain of its soul. When I collect the fresh blood of an animal or fish, I will drain some of it first on the ground or in the water to "give it back." The natives believed that by doing this and covering the blood up with fallen leaves, the animal would rise back up from the ground reborn and unharmed.

After washing and tending to the parts, I will tell the spirit how the fetish will be used. Sometimes, they wish to help a bit spiritually, while other times they wish to rest in peace. This is especially common with roadkill. Every piece of animal I use is always done with consent, because I wouldn't want just anybody taking anything they wanted from my dead body. I wouldn't care what it was for. They deserve the same respect. In Appalachia, hunters and fishers try to never waste anything. You can go to any flea market, antique store, or fair around here and you'll always find somebody selling hides and bones.

"Waste not, want not" is a strong saying here, which is why you always hear about "hillbillies" eating roadkill. Because most folks do— or they used to. They hate seeing a deer, possum, or something going to waste just rotting on the side of the road. However you collect the

---

[4] James Mooney, *Myths of the Cherokee: Extract from the Nineteenth Annual Report of the Bureau of American Ethnology* (Washington, D.C.: Government Printing Office, 1902).

parts, do so ethically and with consent. I always offer tobacco leaves or smoke for them, which usually sells them on the whole thing. But sometimes even the most sacred plant in the mountains can't persuade them enough. They just want to rest. The animals I do work with only ask for a bit of tobacco and water every now and then. They are simple because they lived simple lives: eat, drink, survive. That's it. They didn't have taste for cakes, rum, or cornbread. Although raccoons may be a bit different and somewhat picky.

Sometimes your connection to an animal will grow stagnant or die out. I take this as a sign that they're ready to retire. That is when I'll take them out and bury them with tobacco and prayers, placing stones over the grave of fur, bones, or skin, and singing "Auld Lang Syne."

Mind you, none of this is documented tradition; it's simply how I do things and how I grew into the work. I hate animal abuse and their deaths being in vain. I make sure that I source materials that have been ethically procured. Aside from the humane aspect, you don't want to work with a spirit that has trauma attached to it. Below is a list of animals and the assistance they can possibly bring.

Coyote/Wolf: Protection from enemies, witchcraft, and unwanted guests. A spiritual guard dog. The teeth and claws can be carried for protection. It is called for frostbite because it is among a number who stay out in the snow with no consequences.

Deer: Buck and doe parts can be used in works for fertility, love, lust, and spiritual communication. Smack deer antlers together while calling on their spirit or some other entity. "Buck's blood" was used in works of love, lust, and libido. ("Buck's blood" refers to the popular alcoholic drink Jägermeister, which is still believed to contain male deer blood in its recipe of roots. My father used to carry a shot of it with him when he was hunting. Later, I came to find out that the logo is inspired by Saint Hubertus, patron of hunting.) The Cherokee recognized the white deer as Little Deer, their chief, who would come to a hunted deer as it died and ask if the hunter prayed first. If not, Little Deer would strike the hunter with rheumatism.

Raccoon: Work with raccoons for prosperity, especially in times of financial trouble, by hiding a scrap of coonskin in a jar of beans, positioned so the skin cannot be seen. When you cash your first paycheck of the month, go get it in cash first. The last bill the teller lays down is the one you need. In all four corners and the center of the bill, right "fruits." Add to the jar a pinch of salt, a piece of cornbread, and that money. Keep this hidden high up somewhere in the home, as long as it's secret and above your head, to keep your luck and money up.

Turkey: Although they're the ugliest bird in the forest, they're the most promiscuous. Turkey bones and beards, in Appalachia and the Ozarks, were hidden under truck seats and beds to gain the sexual affection of a person.

Vulture: As the scavenger who can consume anything, it was seen as the chief animal in guarding against disease and witchcraft. Hang the feathers above the door for protection.

Rabbit: This animal aids with fertility, clearing the evil eye, and promotes good fortune through the left hind foot.

Snake: Snake oil helps with arthritis, pain, and other general issues; and the bones or skin, powdered, are used to cross people up or bind them to something or someplace.

Cardinal: This bird's feathers are used for love, marriage, ancestor work, and to protect children.

Woodpecker: This bird's feathers are carried for luck and to attain your wishes.

Chicken: Black feathers from this bird are used for removing and placing tricks. The rooster's feathers will always triumph over anything done with a black hen's feathers because they're naturally dominant. Black rooster and hen blood was also used to cure shingles and other ailments. I take a bundle of black rooster tail feathers and bind them around a stick to make a "conjure duster," as I call it, to sweep from head to toe while praying Psalm 23.

Bat: The heart, blood dried on a hankie, or the leather wing was carried for good luck, especialy in matters of employment and gambling.

The relationship between the animals and the mountaineer is deep. Aside from this, animal spirits aren't seen as being prone to guiding or giving individuals help, as if they were assigned to help in spiritual matters for the person throughout life. However, many people still believe that God and the angels use animals to give signs and omens based on their behavior and how they appear, either in person in a certain location or in the dream world. These symbolic and sometimes factual tales lead to certain parts of the beast being given authority and power in areas of life.

SAINTS AND PROPHETS

Religion in Appalachia is a paradox: some doctrines are treated loosely, while others are hard-and-fast rules to follow. I've known plenty of people who'd get drunk over the weekend and go to church on Sunday for forgiveness, although Nana always said the Lord quits forgiving after awhile.

Since I grew up in a Freewill Baptist home, I will speak from that viewpoint first. Saints aren't regarded in the same way as you may be used to with the Catholic Church. For Baptists, saints aren't believed to possess any more power than the living who have faith. A man calling to the Almighty and the one going to a prophet for specific advice or help are the same, because power comes from the Creator either way. In church, we were always taught in hacking and hollering preaching about the power invested in prophets such as Moses, Peter, and David. We were also reminded of the words of Christ when he said anyone with faith could do the same as he did and more so.

In the hooting and hollering, Papaw would kick his leg out in the Spirit, talking about the struggles that God put them through and how he calls upon the least of his own: the barren woman to give rise to a nation or a stuttering man to speak the Word. (When Papaw was in the Spirit he did stuff like that. Other people sometimes do similar things—roll on the floor, speaking in tongues, run around. It's kind of like being possessed by the Holy Ghost.) This belief is the basis behind such practices as faith healing, casting out evil spirits, using prayer cloths, praying down the Devil, and calling something from the Lord. The Appalachian Protestant and Baptist churches also teach that those born in the body of Christ are saints, but the mountaineer is too humble for that. We're always at the mercy of the Creator, always unworthy, which is reflected in the dying practices we spoke of in chapter 5 where you're to enter heaven with your eyes closed in an act of humility. Following is a list of saints and prophets. I encourage you to learn everything you can about them and develop a relationship with those that call to you.

Moses

Moses was a prophet who set his people free from Egypt, parted the Red Sea, turned wood into a serpent, and brought plagues over the land. People pray to him to set folks free from alcoholism and addiction, from the sins and struggles that hold them down, and to part the seas for their escape from circumstances "by the Blood." Call upon Moses to remove conjurings, to set you free from unwanted situations or people, or to impose justice, since he was the vessel for God's commandments.

I remember one time a traveling preacher came to the church. I was maybe four or five years old, but I remember he was speaking about Moses using his staff to part the seas and beat his enemies. The man walked with a cane, and he equated his cane with the strength of the Lord, on which he can lean for assistance in rebuking spirits of pain that festered in his joints and in getting rid of folks who weren't good for nothing.

Moses enjoys offerings of whiskey, cornbread, and tobacco. In working with him, you can also set out a framed picture on your working space. Offerings and pictures of prophets and saints aren't traditional and are very rarely seen in Appalachia aside from Catholic households. However, I'm sure you are familiar already with the loose strings of Appalachian Christianity that place symbolic power on the backs of certain birds, beasts, and natural occurrences regardless of whether a biblical ground is present. It's all about faith, and sometimes it's better to have company.

Simon Peter

Peter, a former fisherman, was one of Jesus's first disciples. Peter was even freed from prison by an angel. The story goes that Herod the king arrested Peter, put him in prison, and assigned four squads of soldiers to keep him, intending to bring him before the people after Passover. But the church prayed for him, and one night while Peter was sleeping, help arrived.

> *Suddenly an angel of the Lord appeared and a light shone in the cell. He tapped Peter on the side and woke him up, saying, "Get up quickly." And the chains fell off his wrists. "Get dressed and put on your sandals," said the angel. Peter did so, and the angel told him, "Wrap your cloak around you and follow me." (Acts 12:7–8)*

In the Bible, Peter is found to be gentle yet firm. He was told by Christ that he held the keys of heaven and had the power to bind things on earth and in heaven. Because of this, he can be called upon for good fishing, healing, divination in the spirit, court work, to keep away the law, to have thieves return stolen goods, or to catch a criminal by praying to him to "bind him on earth and in heaven, Peter, bind it! Peter, bind it! Peter, bind it!"[5] If you're not good at openly praying, recite this verse:

> *And I will give unto thee the keys of the kingdom of heaven: and whatsoever thou shalt bind on earth shall be bound in heaven: and whatsoever thou shalt loose on earth shall be loosed in heaven. (Matthew 16:19)*

Others may work with Peter for protection, but I never really got that feeling from Scripture, as he swings back and forth from one

---

[5] Prayers to Saint Peter for binding people are widespread and occur in charms given in *The Long Lost Friend* by John Hohman, or in the *Albertus Magnus: Egyptian Secrets*, which was widely used in northern Appalachia for Pennsylvania Dutch folk healing practices.

extreme to the next. He was a courageous soldier in battle who could take physical attacks well; however, he became cowardly in the face of persecution or ridicule and physical attacks from behind.

Since Peter keeps the Gates of Heaven, he is also associated with the crossroads that act as a gateway between the living and the dead. For this he can close or open the roads before you or another. To conjure him, get a glass of red wine or whiskey as an offering with a Bible, a candle, and two keys. Tie these keys together with red string to make a cross. Set these out on a table. Light the candle, and then make four knocks on the table in a cross pattern, going from top to bottom and then right to left, to open the space to him. Pray to him with your petitions or prayers. Once done, knock again four times in reverse, going from bottom to top, left to right to close the way. Tell him also to close the way to guard against any haints lurking around.

Saint John the Baptist

The Baptist Church is based on the teachings and practices of baptizing. Therefore, John the Baptist holds a special place in the Southern Baptist mind—even for those who aren't religious. John represents the end goal of a life of struggle and pain in the mountains, as foretold through Isaiah 40:3:

> *The voice of him that crieth in the wilderness, Prepare ye the way of the Lord, make straight in the desert a highway for our God.*

In the spirit of John the Baptist, folks were baptized in rivers and creeks, just as he had done long before baptismal pools were built in churches. If you ever lose faith in God, light a white candle and go to the river. Immerse your feet in the water, sit on the bank facing east while holding the lit candle, and pray to John to help you restore your faith. This is helpful especially when you just can't bring yourself to talk to God. In this way, you are speaking with someone who used to be human and went through trials just as you have. It makes it a little easier. For offerings, give corn, moonshine, Balm of Gilead (a bud of a flowering tree in the mountains used in remedies), and water.

Saint Jude

While most of Appalachia has historically been Baptist or Protestant, we do have a small, yet strong Catholic presence, with roots going back to the pilgrims. However, most of this population remains up north in upper Appalachia and has had a large influence in the development of Pennsylvania Dutch Powwow, remnants of which have trickled down into the Blue Ridge Mountains and surrounding areas.

Some traditional Catholic saints are known everywhere here, and Saint Jude, patron of lost causes and the desperate, is one of them. Saint Jude candles are everywhere in grocery stores, pharmacies, and gas stations. Grocery stores sell out of them often regardless of the small Catholic population in Appalachia.

Named the "patron of impossibility," Saint Jude is a reminder that with the Creator all things are possible, even the resolution of the most hopeless of matters, which may explain his popularity among Appalachian Americans. Although he isn't recognized with this same power or status in the Baptist Church, his presence in moonshine country and globally cannot be expected to have kept its influence confined around the regional folk medicines and magic of Appalachia.

Saint Jude is called upon for help in dire situations and to protect you from your enemies. He will never do harm to anyone, but he will confuse your enemies possibly—because Saint Jude was bashed to death in the head with a club. A consequence of this: you will want to be very specific in your prayers to him. Don't tell him you need money for bills; give him an exact amount. He enjoys offerings of tobacco, chocolates, bread, pennies, and public thanks, such as an ad in the newspaper.

The Madonna

A couple of years ago, we lived down the road from Saint Mary's Catholic Church. It was situated on a huge piece of land occupied by windflowing fields and a few pine trees. You have to take a winding road going by some woods to get to the church, and along that road is a grove dedicated to the Blessed Mother with a large statue.

The mother of Christ holds importance for many people, even non-Catholics. She is included in many charms, especially those reigning from Germany that were recorded by John Hohman in *The Long Lost Friend*. Other times, Mary is simply used as a symbol, as in the case of this formula to ease arthritis: "As Mary will not bear another child, may this [body part] bear no more pain."[6] This draws a likeness between the eternal status of Mary (no longer bearing children) to the body doing the same: no longer bearing pain.

Most often, the Madonna is turned to in times of childbirth with remedies and formulas that seem to stem primarily from the West of Ireland. These formulas often told stories of the holy family or simply dialogues between Christ and His mother. An infamous amulet used by the Irish was a "Mary's bean" (*Merremia discoidesperma*). During times of struggling labor, the women would hold it in their hands while praying to the Virgin, "As you were delivered of Christ, and Anna was delivered of you; as Elizabeth was delivered of John the Baptist: deliver me of this child and let me be well." Leave her offerings of water, flowers, chocolates, and tobacco.

---

[6] Variations of this can be found in Hohman's *The Long Lost Friend*.

My mother always preferred the Virgin of Guadeloupe, the most famous apparition of the Virgin from Mexico and the most common candle in our grocery stores here. I've prayed to her for everything from financial issues and blessings to protection from enemies and safe travel.

CASTING APPLE SEEDS
Spelling and Fortune-Telling

The mind of the mountaineer was filled with fear of the unknown in their new homeland in the mountains. This fear, coupled with a strong faith, furthered the progression of superstition in Appalachia, whether carried over from the Old World or simply coined up. The granny witches and power doctors (often the only medical help available within days of travel) held to a tradition of discerning God's will by following signs and listening to the Spirit. We've seen previously how the formation of roots, star signs, and the weather can foretell fate.

But divination has deeper and more complex roots in these hills than those already covered. Fortunes of work and love, the identity of a husband's mistress, a thief, or an enemy can be found out. Back in the day, gypsies would often travel up and down the mountain range. Some of them were from the usual places such as Italy or Hungary, while others were from Scotland or Britain. They employed the usual playing cards and crystal ball. Some historical root workers in Appalachia did use crystal balls, with one example being Ed Mctear of South Carolina. He was a sheriff who first got into the work in order to understand certain cases more. These cases included the famous Dr. Buzzard, one of the most renowned hoodoos in North American history.

Aside from the usual long layouts of cards and crystal gazing, Appalachian divination methods primarily follow probability like "yes or no." These are at the bottom of the divination pole since they are the simplest methods found.

YES OR NO, IS OR AIN'T SO

In chapter 2, I mentioned using an egg to determine if a woman is with child. For this, a fresh egg is rubbed counterclockwise over the woman's womb, right beneath her naval. The Lord's Prayer is recited, ending with a prayer like, "Lord, you give dreams and visions of righteousness for Your name. Show me how it is here." The woman then blows on the egg, and it is dropped into a clear glass of water and then read. If it sinks to the bottom of the glass, she is "heavy" with child. If it floats, she isn't pregnant. Oftentimes, this will predict a pregnancy: if the woman is not pregnant at the moment but the egg still sinks, the woman will very likely become pregnant within six months.

Playing cards can also be used for this. Shuffle a deck three times and draw three cards. The black suits mean no and the red suits mean yes, so the probability is determined by the suit of two out of the three cards.

You can also utilize the "scattering" forms of divination, which entail tossing sunflower or apple seeds on a handkerchief after whispering your question into them. If the seeds are evenly spaced out after landing, it means yes; but if they land in groups or "clods," it is a no.

FORMATIONS AND PATTERNS

Another method calls for placing something in a particular place or environment and interpreting letters or other signs formed. This is usually done with corn kernels that are thrown in a circle drawn into the dirt, and the resulting patterns are meditated on to find letters, shapes, or other patterns.

Reading coffee grounds is also included in this. A cup of coffee is drunk until the last sip, at which point a teaspoon of coffee grounds is added to the cup. Breathe three times into the cup, and cover it with a saucer. Then pass the cup and saucer over the head in a circle three times and quickly turn it upside down so the mouth of the cup rests on the plate. Once all the liquid has drained, read the grounds inside the cup. An *X* shows a blockage. Two parallel trails of dots means a busy or tough path. The shape of a dog means death, a heart is someone you love, and so on.

Here's a formula I use to find someone out—a future love, a thief, or an enemy. Set out a large basin of water, enough to hold about a gallon. Take 7, 13, or 21 toothpicks and lay them individually on the surface of the water with your right hand. (The number of toothpicks you use is individual taste; however, the number is traditionally odd. Seven is associated with fortune and luck; thirteen is famous for its connections to witchcraft. Twenty-one has never been explained to me—it is simply a number I was taught had importance, so I use it and it works.) Once all of the toothpicks are in the water, cover it with a white towel and raise one end just enough to whisper into it, "In the name of the Father, Son, and Holy Ghost, tell me what I wish to see. You tell of all things in righteousness and by Your Word have proclaimed anything asked in Your name will be done. So tell me _____." Then blow three times on the surface of the water. Leave the pot by the bed, and in the morning the toothpicks will have formed the person's initials. You can also practice this on a smaller scale using 7 toothpicks and a white porcelain bowl of water left by the bed while you sleep.

SAMUELS AND JACK-BALLS

A samuel is a weighted bag of curios suspended on a red cord whose movements are interpreted to see things backstage about a situation. It's basically an ol' country pendulum crafted from roots and red flannel. It is called a samuel, to my knowledge, because of the witch calling Samuel's spirit up for Saul in the Bible:

1 Samuel 28:3–20

> 3 *Now Samuel was dead, and all Israel had lamented him, and buried him in Ramah, even in his own city. And Saul had put away those that had familiar spirits, and the wizards, out of the land.*

> 4 *And the Philistines gathered themselves together, and came and pitched in Shunem: and Saul gathered all Israel together, and they pitched in Gilboa.*

> 5 *And when Saul saw the host of the Philistines, he was afraid, and his heart greatly trembled.*

> 6 *And when Saul enquired of the Lord, the Lord answered him not, neither by dreams, nor by Urim, nor by prophets.*

> 7 *Then said Saul unto his servants, Seek me a woman that hath a familiar spirit, that I may go to her, and enquire of her. And his servants said to him, Behold, there is a woman that hath a familiar spirit at Endor.*

> 8 *And Saul disguised himself, and put on other raiment, and he went, and two men with him, and they came to the woman by night: and he said, I pray thee, divine unto me by the familiar spirit, and bring me him up, whom I shall name unto thee.*

> 9 *And the woman said unto him, Behold, thou know-est what Saul hath done, how he hath cut off those that have familiar spirits, and the wizards, out of the land:*

wherefore then layest thou a snare for my life, to cause me to die?

10 And Saul sware to her by the Lord, saying, As the Lord liveth, there shall no punishment happen to thee for this thing.

11 Then said the woman, Whom shall I bring up unto thee? And he said, Bring me up Samuel.

12 And when the woman saw Samuel, she cried with a loud voice: and the woman spake to Saul, saying, Why hast thou deceived me? for thou art Saul.

13 And the king said unto her, Be not afraid: for what sawest thou? And the woman said unto Saul, I saw gods ascending out of the earth.

14 And he said unto her, What form is he of? And she said, An old man cometh up; and he is covered with a mantle. And Saul perceived that it was Samuel, and he stooped with his face to the ground, and bowed himself.

15 And Samuel said to Saul, Why hast thou disquieted me, to bring me up? And Saul answered, I am sore distressed; for the Philistines make war against me, and God is departed from me, and answereth me no more, neither by prophets, nor by dreams: therefore I have called thee, that thou mayest make known unto me what I shall do.

16 Then said Samuel, Wherefore then dost thou ask of me, seeing the Lord is departed from thee, and is become thine enemy?

17 And the Lord hath done to him, as he spake by me: for the Lord hath rent the kingdom out of thine hand, and given it to thy neighbour, even to David:

18 Because thou obeyedst not the voice of the Lord, nor executedst his fierce wrath upon Amalek, therefore hath the Lord done this thing unto thee this day.

19 Moreover the Lord will also deliver Israel with thee into the hand of the Philistines: and to morrow shalt thou and thy sons be with me: the Lord also shall deliver the host of Israel into the hand of the Philistines.

20 Then Saul fell straightway all along on the earth, and was sore afraid, because of the words of Samuel: and there was no strength in him; for he had eaten no bread all the day, nor all the night.

The spirit the Bible identifies as Samuel told no lie, for everything came to pass. Further examining the use of this charm, we can also connect the birth and naming of Samuel:

Wherefore it came to pass, when the time was come about after Hannah had conceived, that she bare a son, and called his name Samuel, saying, Because I have asked him of the Lord. (1 Samuel 1:20)

Samuel was also a just judge, and anointed kings such as David. Samuel told the truth of God handing over Israel and of Saul's death when he was called up through a medium, one of the most forbidden acts named by Scripture. Because of this it's said your samuel cannot lie and must always tell the way things are or will be; and your samuel will not work for other people. The name Samuel also meant "the name is God," or "God is lifted up," further adding to its power and roots in

Scripture. Another name was a jack-ball or simply jack. You can name it anything you want, but samuel is what my family calls it.

To make a samuel, bring a 4 inch by 4 inch piece of white or red flannel to a Sunday church sermon and lay it open on your lap during the service. Then lay the cloth on a table and place a pinch each of salt and tobacco in the center of the fabric. Two roots are used in this samuel: one thin root of bearded iris (*Iris germanica*) that ran east and one root of Mayapple (*Podophyllum peltatum*) that ran south, each one cut fresh to the length of your thumbs. Bind these with twine to form a cross and lay them over the salt and tobacco. Place a stone from a churchyard over that. Knot a piece of red yarn 13 inches in length three times over itself to make a larger knot, and then tuck it into the center hole. Gather the four corners of the fabric and tie a knot tight with another piece of red yarn.

If you like, a simpler samuel can be made without the roots.

When you have your samuel, call out to it, saying something like,

> *Samuel! Samuel! Wake up now. In the name of God the Father, God the Son, and God the Holy Ghost, you're gonna tell me what's right and how things are. You are only tied to me under the Most High and will tell His word on things, anything I want to know.*

To work it, hold it still by the end of the yarn. Always call it by its name, saying something like,

> *Alright now, Samuel, tell me—is there somebody working trouble for me? Are they shooting or conjuring me?*

If it trembles, or seems to shake or jump, trouble is coming. If it waves from left to right or stands still, that means no. If it swings to and fro or in circles, it means yes. And if it simply remains in the same place and turns or spins, it means there's more to the situation than you know, or you have not asked the right question. The samuel will only tell you the truth in direct answers, so word your questions carefully.

OTHER PENDULUM DEVICES AND DOWSING

One of the most famous southern tricks using a pendulum is determining if a woman is pregnant and what the child's sex will be. The woman's wedding ring was suspended from a red string or seven hairs taken from the crown of her head. Writing this here, I wondered what would be used if the woman wasn't married, so I called my mother. She said there wasn't a substitute since is wasn't really heard of for a girl to be pregnant out of wedlock. However, the wedding ring of the girl's mother could be used. The pendulum is held aloft by another person right over the naval of the laying woman. Movement back and forth meant is was a boy or no, she wasn't pregnant; circular patterns meant it was a girl or yes, she was pregnant.

As recent as two generations ago, "water witches" were well known, and it was customary for one to help you find underground water in order to dig a well, or even to help find lost items, treasure, or people. My great-great-grandfather Oscar was a water witch. A forked stick from a willow, cherry, pear, hazel, or hickory tree, was used, held by the two prongs outward, fists down, with one stoke pointing up toward the sky. The specific type of wood used was solely up to the family. Dowsing rods were always taken from a branch pointing to the east during the full moon, as that's the time all water is being pulled on, and it would likewise help the stick be pulled to the water source.

The prongs are pulled apart and kept at just the right tension before snapping. Held like this, the dowser marks where they began and begins to walk in various directions. As they approach water underground, the stick will begin to bob or wiggle, and as soon as they make it to the full source (the place to dig the well) it will point straight out or "jump down."

According to my Nana, Papaw Oscar would take the measurement between the place he started and where he found the source, and that would be how far down you'd need to dig to get to the water.

PLAYING CARDS

From a very young age, I remember my family using playing cards from the dollar store for games like rummy, roulette, spades, and solitaire. As one of the most used forms of divination, playing cards have a long line of tradition in Appalachia. Each number and suit is related to an event or a person. They are read in multiple ways just like tarot cards, and some families have their own spreads and ways of cutting the cards.

My mother is the one who taught me how to use playing cards for divination. I vaguely remember sitting in the kitchen with her; the only light was the stove, with all the windows and doors open that summer night to let the heat and cigarette smoke out. She'd flip the cards out on the counter and tell me whatever was about to happen. I still use the deck she taught me on.

I will go over the simplest way she taught me to read the cards for a general overview of how things are in your life. You need a new deck of cards, reserved only for reading—it's important to keep reading cards and game cards separate. Some families will have a deck solely for themselves, and if it's read for other people then that person must supply a brand-new deck or simply use one from their own home. (Now, decks do get old with time, and sometimes cards are lost. The one I use, the deck I learned on, is composed of cards from at least five different decks. Anytime Mama lost a card, she'd grab that same card from an unused deck and add it to her reading one.)

Shuffle the deck three times, then knock the top three times. Part the cards into two stacks and hold them to your mouth and breathe on them. Then shuffle the deck again. Starting from the top of the deck, flip each and every card over so it's faceup. When you get two of the same card in a row, set those aside and keep them in the order they came up. Keep doing this until you reach the last card. Then turn to the doubles you have gathered and interpret them as follows:

Kings represent money and business. If they are of different colors, expect some delays or losses. The king of spades, facing the right, is especially foreboding in this area. Same-color suits predict favorable finances or good luck in the home or business.

Queens represent lovers. If they are facing to the left, they are loyal; to the right means they aren't telling the truth or they are hiding something. If both cards are red, it enforces that they are loyal; if they are black suits, they further the deceit. If the suits are different colors, there is difficulty in the relationship. If one is the queen of spades, there's been infidelity. Different colors can also mean a different lover, such as a new person or one other than the current lover.

Jacks represent jealousy from other people. Someone doesn't always keep you in good thoughts, and they can be further found based on the suits. Matching-colored suits shows it is a close friend who's jealous, while different-colored suits means it is likely a stranger or enemy. The enemy can be seen for sure should the jack of spades rear its ugly head in any combination. This can also be indicative of the "pewter" (evil eye) being present.

Tens represent dreams and desires either fulfilled or thwarted based on other cards. If they're both red, their endeavors will prosper; if they're both black, they'll fall short or be interrupted. If the pair is different colors, this can show indecisiveness or hesitation.

Nines mean trouble, turmoil, or strife is coming. In a reading to figure out the cause of a situation, this can also mean witchcraft or conjuring has occurred. If they are both red, then there's trouble in the home, in a relationship, or with one's health or business; if they're both black, there's trouble in spiritual matters. If they are different colors, then its folk name "the pallbearers" comes into play, meaning something needs to be taken care of—loose ends need to be tied up or someone needs to "bury the hatchet."

Eights mean sorrow is coming. This can also be related to simple depression, breakups, job loss, etc. For example, two different-color kings, two sixes, and two eights would propose a possible job and financial loss. The colors of each would further determine the severity of the meaning.

Sevens mean there is protection and safety under "God's lucky number." Sevens also represent tears, worry, waiting, and blood, though. If a spade comes out, then you are at risk. Two sevens, one a spade, can also mean you have lost something dear.

Sixes represent bad news, particularly if the six of spades is in the pair. If it is the left card of the two, then it isn't too serious; if it is on the right side, the bad news is serious business. The colors of the suits will determine what person the news will come from, as explained below for the fives.

Fives mean good news is coming. If the pair is red and black, the news will come from a person of the opposite sex; if the suits are the same color, it will be from someone of the same sex.

Fours represent travel, either coming or going. Different suits mean the person will travel to "strange ground," while matching colors represent some place you've been before.

Threes foretell bad luck, based on what cards they are paired with and how it will come. If a pair of different-colored fours appears with a pair of black threes, it is a warning against travel or large crowds, pointing to possible arguments, accidents, or violence with a four of spades present. Otherwise, it will be trouble with family for hearts, with friends for diamonds, and with business for clubs.

Twos represent good fortune. Again, further information is determined by the other pairs of cards present.

Aces represent love. It could be love of friends, family, or lovers. If the pair is a heart and a spade, there's heartbreak or it won't last. A spade and a club indicates abuse or addiction. A heart with a club means they fight too much or there's distance. A heart and a diamond means they're a match, but there are some rough edges. A diamond and a club means all is well. Finally, a spade and diamond mean an ending or death.

To close the reading, shuffle the deck thrice, make the sign of the cross over them, and smack the deck.

GAZING

Gazing, also known as scrying, can be done in a number of ways: looking into a well or bowl of water, gazing into a mirror with a candle over your right shoulder, or watching smoke and the way things burn.

In Ireland, the Celts held the hazelnut to be a symbol and charm of knowledge and wisdom, but also of love—and they'd burn it as a form of scrying. On St. John's Eve, St. John's Day, Halloween, or Pentecost, make a fire in the hearth and take two hazelnuts named for each person in the potential relationship. Toss the nuts into the fire, and if they both burn smoothly down to ash, then the relationship will work and may even result in marriage. If they pop, break, or jump out, then it will never last.

The same kind of method is employed with sheaves of wheat, barley, or corn fodder: a certain number of bundles are laid on hot coals or embers one at a time. The way they burn and the behavior of the smoke is read to predict the future or the outcome of events happening elsewhere. Even and good burns are best, but if the fodder burns quickly or refuses to burn all the way, it means something bad (the person is "shot," they won't get better from the sickness, etc., depending on the situation). (Being "shot" is another term for being conjured or worked on in Appalachia.) If the fodder lights into a flame, the spirits are showing you that something is happening right now. If the flame moves toward you, you'll hear of it soon. If it moves away from you or to the left, the event will not be for the better; but if it moves to the right and near you, it will be for the better.

The duration of the flame should be taken into account also: the longer it remains and moves, the greater the influence. If the smoke drifts to the east or south, it is good; if it's to the west or north, it is bad. Billows and tornado-like movements in the smoke mean great outer influence (such as witchcraft or a third party); partings in the line of smoke represent a disconnect or something not being accounted for (this usually happens because the client has withheld important information from those performing the working); and if the smoke falls to the ground, the situation is helpless.

One method employed on Halloween night was to peel an apple, and while holding the big toe of your right foot in the fist of your left hand, toss the apple peel over your left shoulder. The peel will land in the form of your future love's initials.

To gaze with water, use water from a well in a white porcelain bowl. Get a bundle of burning chicken feathers, and smudge yourself and waft the smoke over the surface of the water. (Chickens have a long history in assisting mountain folk in predictions and divination. They heralded the new day and the rising sun, and in Appalachia they were watched to predict rain, good weather, luck for the day before heading out, love interests that were true, and even death.)

Sit while gazing into the water and recite the following three times:

> *In the name of the Father, the Son, and the Holy Spirit,*
> *As far as the east is from the west,*
> *Let me see _____.*

Then gaze into the water to watch for pictures that may form. Look *through* the water and bowl; bring yourself out of focus and let everything flow. Don't try to focus on your inquiry, just let the vines and weeds of your mind unfurl and you'll eventually find your answer. You always will. You can also use this same blessing and simply rub the water over your eyes as you retire for bed. Write down the verses that follow and place them under your bed in a bowl of salted water to dream the truth of the situation:

> *Howbeit when he, the Spirit of truth, is come, he will*
> *guide you into all truth: for he shall not speak of himself;*
> *but whatsoever he shall hear, that shall he speak: and he*
> *will shew you things to come.*
>
> *He shall glorify me: for he shall receive of mine, and shall*
> *shew it unto you.*
>
> *All things that the Father hath are mine: therefore said*
> *I, that he shall take of mine, and shall shew it unto you.*
>
> *(John 16:13–15)*

Some old granny women and power men have been recorded in folklore as having the ability to see or "spell" things that have happened or will happen. ("Spelling" is another Appalachian term used to describe practices of fortune telling.) One such woman, Mammy

Wise, was said to have predicted the Civil War because she saw a star shoot from the north and hit a star in the south, indicating trouble was stirring between the North and the South. Oral tradition says her eyes "went dead" and her hands shook when she peered off and saw things. People from all over North Carolina, Tennessee, Virginia, and elsewhere went to see her to find out who stole what, who killed who, or what messages the stars held.

I'm not sure if the phrase "went dead" meant her eyes rolled back into her head like a Hollywood cliché or they simply glazed over and stared off at nothing. I've never heard of a dead man's eyes rolling around his head, so I presume the phrase meant the latter. This is the only historical account of someone gazing off to see things that I've found. The accounts I've witnessed are my Nana and her late husband, the preacher man.

9

STOLEN FLOWERS
Tools and Supplies

The tools used in this work are oftentimes already in people's kitchens. The one thing I remember about my Nana Trivett's kitchen is the flowers she kept. They were never given to her or bought; they were stolen. She'd pick a rose from a neighbor's bush down the road and bring it home to root or pluck a stem from a plant at the garden center. She always said stolen flowers grew the best, although she loved flowers of any kind. But she will never thank you for them, or they'll die. Stolen flowers bring love and luck to the household, symbolizing the simple beliefs that keep the family going. Under Nana's kitchen window was her junk drawer, which held basically everything in this chapter.

The tools used in this work are common, so no need to worry about buying expensive things. And should you be without a certain tool, make use of something you already have. There ain't no sense in buying something I recommend when you may have something better. The old folks didn't have botanicas or new age stores they could just hop on down to for supplies, and I reckon they wouldn't step foot in one anyway. Instead, they used what they had, and if all they had was scraps of newspaper, yarn, and a candle, then so be it. They made it work. All that said, while these tools aren't essential, they will make the work easier for you.

Mortar and Pestle

The mortar and pestle has been used in medicine and magic for thousands of years. Its ancestor was much different than the modern form of bowl and stick. Different cultures across the globe would grind their herbs down between two stones until they were finely sifted or powdered. I have one grindstone that I created myself: a large flat rock with a circular indention and a palm-sized river stone that fits perfectly into the groove. In my opinion, a grindstone is easier on your hands.

Don't be surprised if you get sores on your hand from the mortar and pestle, or at the least arthritis. Don't hurt yourself trying to get your herbs or other materials to the right consistency. Just pick out the parts that won't grind and return them to the earth. Over the years, I've used many mortars and pestles made from all kinds of materials—olive wood, aluminum, marble, concrete. My personal favorite is concrete, as it works best and doesn't stain easily, like white marble does. If you do get a heavy concrete one, a word to the wise: hold it tightly. I've had many a scare of a broken toe!

Trowel/Shovel

A trowel is a multipurpose, must-have tool if you plan on growing your own herbs. When digging for roots, burying works, or getting dirt, it makes the work easier for you and your hands.

Broom

In Appalachia, the broom is surrounded by superstitions. If a freestanding broom falls with no one around, unexpected company is on the way. If you sweep over someone's feet, they'll go to jail; sweep under their feet, and they'll never marry. There's also the tradition of jumping the broom at weddings for luck or fertility.

Aside from local superstition, the broom has a long history in witchcraft. The broom is used to periodically sweep the porch and lawn to get rid of any tricks that may have been placed on the property, especially at the edge. To cleanse the house of illness or evil, anoint the bristles of the broom with holy water and cast some blessed salt, then sweep the house from the back to the front, eventually sweeping the salt out the door. When a troublesome person leaves your home, throw salt and pepper in their tracks on the porch and sweep it off so they will never return. The broom can also be placed upside down, bristles up, after someone leaves, to keep them away for good.

Gloves

Gloves will protect your skin from getting stuck on plants with thorns, such as roses or thistle blooms. While gloves aren't required, they can save you some time and hurt. Of course, they aren't mandatory; I've used a scrap of deerskin to guard my palm while picking herbs.

Knives

Knives are a staple in all forms of witchcraft. In Appalachian folk magic, one can use anything from a kitchen knife to a pocketknife. Like brooms, knives are surrounded by superstition. When a bad storm is approaching, go to the south side of the house and drive the hilt of a knife into the earth with the blade pointing up and facing away from the home. This is said to cut the storm or tornado in half.

One should never close a pocketknife that someone else opened or it will bring bad luck. And if someone gives you a knife of any kind, you must offer a penny to "buy" it. Otherwise, the knife could severe your relationship. Knives are used for protection, cutting away pain or fear, and to remedy wounds they cause.

Yarn and Ribbon

For many works, you will need string or yarn of some kind. Back in the day bailing twine was often used, as sewing twine was reserved to repair clothes. My favorite material is hemp cord, although I often hoard all types of string in my kitchen drawer. The most common color used is red. The grannies would make a red dye from madder or bloodroot to dye the cords. Yarn, ribbon, and string are used to tie up sachets, bind packets, and hang charms, and can even act as charms themselves.

Rags and Hankies

You will also need different types of fabric. Back in my grandmother's day, fabric was easy to get but often expensive, so old hand-me-down clothes were washed in the creek or washtub with vinegar and cut up. These scraps were then used to fix up better clothes when they tore and also for making charm bags and doll babies.

Rags can also be used to curse one's enemies, provide healing from illness, conjure up a rainstorm, and catch the morning dew to be used in love and healing works. Normally, it was just a plain old washcloth or kitchen towel that was used again and again over the years for stopping blood or as a compress, as it was thought to get stronger and stronger with each use. Handkerchiefs and flannel were the most common types of fabric used. Flannel was believed to bring good luck all on its own, so most charm bags are crafted with flannel from old shirts.

Jars

You'll need containers to store herbs for later use, and jars, canisters, and bags work well. The mason jar is probably best, as it is airtight and will preserve the herbs' medicine. These should be stored in a dark place away from direct sunlight. I rarely go out and buy boxes of jars.

My herb shelf is filled with recycled jelly and peanut butter jars, mason jars from antique stores and flea markets, and medicine bottles we dug up in the woods.

Pint jars are best, but if space is tight, 8-ounce jars work just fine. If you use new jars, wash them with saltwater first to purify them, and be sure they are completely dry before filling them. The jars also need to be labeled and dated with the day the herb was harvested. The shelf life of leafy and woody herbs is two years, while spices, such as cinnamon or cayenne, have a shelf life of five to ten years. Jars can also take up a lot of room quickly, so if you have lots of different herbs maybe try using plastic or cloth bags instead.

I also keep a basket in the kitchen to dispose of old flower heads, woody herb stems, spent matches, and blessed salt that I've used. This basket is usually emptied on the full moon beneath a tree or buried at a crossroads once it's full. Bury them. Don't throw these discarded bits out or burn them, as we see this as disrespectful—especially if those herbs are spent leftovers from medicine.

Recipe Box or Book

Keep your family's home remedies, superstitions, and recipes in a box or a book. There's no need to remember every word of a charm or every ingredient to a brew for colic: write it down and don't be afraid to turn to it for aid. I have five journals, which I keep together in my kitchen. Each one is filled with old remedies, cures, symptoms of folk illnesses, methods, charms, and so on. most of which can only be understood by me. Like prayers, there are no instructions. I simply use the notes to jog my memory, and then I just know how to work the rest.

Candles and Lamps

Candles and oil lamps gave the only light at night back in the day. In the deep hollers of the mountains, the moon's light barely makes it down past the tree limbs. Likewise, candles and lamps guide the way for this spiritual work.

Candles were rubbed with lard, butter, or oil and rolled in sifted herbs or "loaded" by carving out a hole in the bottom, filling it with the herbs, and sealing it. Lamps were loaded by placing the herbs and things in the basin with the oil. Color symbolism didn't matter here as long as it got the job done. Folks used regular white candles for anything, even cursing, because even a plain white candle can kill you. Back in the day, candles were hand dipped, and I still make my own this way. If you buy yours, wash them in vinegar to cleanse them and put them up until needed. We'll cover candle and lamp work in the next chapter.

10

WHEN THE ROOSTER CROWS
Appalachian Candle Magic, Doll Babies, and Other Trickery

Through the history of these bloodstained hills and the spirits that cry from them, from the memories of ancestors and posey flowers on the grave, we have come to putting this magic to work.

The charms and roots employed by the grannies, doctors, and laymen of the Appalachian hills are many. The old folks used roots, bark, animal parts, and other ingredients readily at hand based on the time and location they worked. We mountaineers are constantly aware of the bit of Creation that surrounds us. Purple and blue mountains enclose our horizons, possums can always be found on the back porch, and the storms that make their way over the mountaintops are sure to let their presence be known.

These mountains are our life. They have cradled our culture for hundreds of years, swallowed willingly the blood and bones of those lost to wars, bad moonshine deals, and illness. They have wrapped our minds around cow fields, creek beds, and good home cooking; but they have also driven some to madness, tight social structures, and deep isolation, luring our ancestors down faery trails, through haunting stories of haints and strange witch-women.

Yet, these are the same hills that offered a breeding ground for the superstitious charms and herbs that healed everything under God's blue sky. The isolation of the mountains gave way to a sustainable system of folk magic and medicine that has endured for hundreds of years by oral tradition through family lines either from mother to son or father to daughter.

Some people, especially those witch doctors and root workers called on for illnesses or court cases, worked and charmed privately at certain spaces in their home set aside for just that. Whether they were altars, shrines, or just plain old worktables set in a shack out back, it didn't matter. Others, like myself, will charm and work just about anywhere. But in this modern age, folks need a place set aside to help them get out of the world built on steel, concrete, and rubber into the world of faith, healing, and power.

THE WORKING SPACE

Much like the ancestor altar, the working space is often simple—a place that the doctor frequently returns to in order to craft charm bags, create medicines, or simply charm something. No fancy items are needed for a good working space. You'll need a space about two to three feet square; this could be a small table, a kitchen counter, or even a hay bale in a barn. I work at the kitchen counter primarily because that is where I keep all of my tools and herbs, but when I'm taking a working to the spirits, I will go to my dresser, where I have established an altar, a meeting place between me and the spirits, be they little folk, angels, saints, or the dead. This altar doesn't need to be permanent, unless you are setting one up to honor a spirit or prophet, in which case you may designate a separate place for it. Otherwise, the place can be a temporary setup.

So, yes, you can pack up your altar or working space when it is not needed. I use everything for this, from the milk crate in the garden or the kitchen counter to a shelf of my bookcase or floor. If it is simply a working area for the time, I will gather the materials needed such as wax, thread, herbs, fabric, or other curios. If it is for divination or blessing with the help of the spirits, then I make sure to set out a couple of candles, a Bible, and a few fresh glasses of water on a white tablecloth or doily. This is the most basic layout and holds everything needed for just about any kind of work.

The candles and lamps help light your way, the Bible is to look at for verses, and the glasses of water act as both an offering and a medium for spirits to communicate through. To the altar, I would also add olive oil, salt, and a white handkerchief. The oil is for anointing: it can be used for any kind of working by praying over it. To do this, get some on your thumb and whisper your prayers over it:

> *God the Father, God the Son, and God the Holy Ghost,*
> *let me be lucky in this game. Let my hands be decked in*
> *gold and my pockets lined with silver. Shroud me with*
> *good fortune and let chance be under my thumb.*

You would then anoint yourself with it for good luck, primarily on the soles of the feet, palms of the hands, and the sides of your neck by those glands the doctors are always probing on.

Salt is common in folk magic the world over, and in all of those places, as well as Appalachia, it's good for just about anything. Nana used to line the front and back doors with salt for protection, or she'd sprinkle it at the four inside corners of the home in a pile and set a penny up on top for good luck and money. "Salt does what you tell it to" is a well-known saying throughout the American South among doctors and layfolk alike.

Finally, the white handkerchief is probably the best symbol that comes to my mind when I think of this work. The handkerchief catches the sweat and blood of hard work; it wipes the tears of empty beer bottles and Sunday sermons indiscriminately. It wraps itself around small heirloom trinkets and drugs, the sacred and the profane. It wipes the hands of working men and the noses of crying babes. As we've seen previously throughout these pages, a handkerchief can be used to divine God's will or defy it with a bullet and some blood.

A handkerchief tied into a knot will stave off evil spirits, and a hankie left open during an Easter Sunday sermon will prove helpful in healing throughout the year; also, any handkerchief left open in a field on St. John's Eve will act as a protective charm against conjuration and haints. However, never give or receive a used handkerchief as a gift, because you will also be receiving the other person's tears and hardships with it. I never go anywhere without my handkerchief, and my Papaw Trivett's is always tucked into his old bible that I use, which is always sat open to Psalm 23.

Here's a simple layout for the working space: cover a table with a white tablecloth and place the Bible in the center, leaving enough room in front to work. Behind the Bible place an oil lamp or candle with a glass of water for the spirits. To the left of the Bible, place other tools or ingredients, or even a vase of flowers. My family has always had posies of herbs and flowers, whether it was for the sick or to simply bring peace to the home. To the right of the Bible, place your hand-kerchief, and to the right of the candle or lamp put your salt, oil, and blessed water. (Regular table salt is fine, but it must come from a new container and can only be used for rootwork and healing—not cooking. The blessed water can be rain or creek water collected at certain times, water from under a bridge that the living and dead cross over, or simply water that has been blessed by a preacher.)

Now that you have a working space, let's learn more about the formulas that will be made over it.

MAKEUP OF THE FORMULAS

While not every charm, remedy, or token of prayer is conducted the same way in Appalachia, there is a pattern to how the acts are carried out. In the same fashion I did with the rites of the mountaineers, I have also created a framework for how the formulas run, although they aren't all employed together in one work every time. These are simply examples of acts and minor usages in the greater methods of the Appalachian magical formulas.

The two main components of the formulas are words and actions: things that are said in conjunction with things that are done. Most formulas, even those small remedies found in Mamaw's recipe box, often begin or end interchangeably with, "in the name of God the Father, the Son, and the Holy Spirit," while other times calling up the Trinity is the entire charm itself.

Depending on the situation, the prayer may act as either a petition or a command; for example, calling upon the Creator for help or telling a disease to leave the body by the name of the Trinity. The spoken verse of a formula can sometimes exert power through recounting Bible stories or characters from the Bible. For example, when you see a solid white horse, spit in your left hand, dig your right heel into the ground, and slam your right fist into your left hand and say,

> *David on a white horse,*
> *Judas on a mule;*
> *David stands as king*
> *and Judas is the fool.*

This tale gives an impression of getting an upper hand in something or having your stock outweigh that of your rival, your "Judas." It's said to bring success and good fortune.

The power of the spoken word makes an important impact here. In many superstitions of Appalachian folklore, we see the opposite of what is said can come to pass, such as not telling a bad dream before breakfast or it will happen. Many mothers warned their children that if they lied about something, it might come true.

This form of watching one's words in charms of healing or other work is also seen with the Cherokee: the medicine people often used their words to not only comfort the patient by telling them the issue is minor but to also make the perpetrator of the disease or curse inferior. In speaking about a snakebite, they would assure the bitten that it was just a frog that had bitten them, taking out not only fear from the person but also power from the attacker by naming it an inferior creature.[7]

The power of the spoken word is also paired with the biblical beliefs that we can do as Christ did in healing the blind with mud or cursing the fig tree, with faith being the only requirement. Oftentimes, after a cleansing or healing, I will tell the person that it's nothing, it ain't there no more, and to go home with their head high and expect change because it's already in their favor. This has even been used to give time frames: oftentimes Papaw, after talking the fire out or curing colic in a baby, would tell someone it would be just fine in three days, after which it was gone.

In contrast, silence is a virtue in some formulas. Prayers are said silently in the mind to not only keep formulas secret but to speak to God personally. Some healers also believed that if they spoke the prayer out loud or if anyone knew what they were saying, then they would lose their power. The significance of silence is also shown with some charms that can only be done in silence, or the performer must remain in silence upon starting the charm until the following sunset.

The gestures in the Appalachian formulas are extremely varied, and only part of them can be fully traced back to their roots in Europe, Africa, or the indigenous tribes of America. The most common tricks employ some form of symbolic action (such as the passing

---

[7] Mooney, "The Swimmer Manuscript."

and transference rites we went over earlier), and other times they simply involve applying a medicine with symbolic hand gestures, such as making the sign of the cross over a sick person or applying a salve in counterclockwise motions. The sign of the cross is one of the most used symbols here besides the X, the circle, the star and the triangle, symbolic of the Trinity. The circle encompasses and traps, while the star is reminiscent of the stars leading to freedom and the one under which Christ was born. To use the circle, write your target's name on a paper and write your petition around their name in a circle, usually in cursive, without lifting the pencil. A pencil without an eraser was often used, showing you will not "go back" on your wish or desire.

The actions and hand movements employed also factor in the directional rites we spoke about and occur when a candle or egg is passed down the torso, arms, and legs for cleansing, or facing east while stating a verse or giving a prayer. This is also done in fire-talking practices where the "talker" blows on the burn, directing their breath away from the patient.

Another action was to write a prayer down on paper, creating a petition, letter, card, or "ticket." You write your name and birthday on the paper three times to connect it to you or someone else if other connections (like hairs, nail clippings, or clothes) aren't available. On either side, draw a cross and place one in the middle of your name and birthdate:

> *+John Doe+Jan 01 1990+*
> *+John Doe+Jan 01 1990+*
> *+John Doe+Jan 01 1990+*

Other times the date will be exchanged for the person's age or location:

> *+John Doe+Knoxville+*

or

+John Doe+89 years of age+

Write the problem down on a strip of cloth or paper, which is struck out and flanked by two sets of three crosses and covered by "INRI," the abbreviation of the title of Christ on the cross.

I.N.R.I.

+ + + ~~Deep Wound on left shoulder~~ + + +

INRI is often added to place more power on the paper and is found used throughout the Appalachian north and south, as well as in the Ozarks and the German-Russian healing practices of the Great Plains.

Another example is for situations involving two or more people with the goal of either harmonizing the relationship or bringing it to ruins. To harmonize, each letter not shared by both names is crossed out with a diagonal slash (/), leaving nothing but matching letters for each name. So in the example below, *m* would be marked off, as would the *D*. Once done, you are left with both names harmonizing with matching letters.

+John Doe Smith+

+Jane Elizabeth Rogers+

These papers are then folded up and added to charms, hidden in the house, worn in the shoe, or nailed to a tree.

When making jack hands, they are the first and primary things added, although they're sometimes the entire charm themselves. Papers are only burned when something needs to be released or removed, never when you are trying to attract or guard. If you are bringing something to you, the paper should be folded toward you. If you are getting rid of something, fold it away from you. Between each fold, turn it clockwise if calling something to you or counterclockwise if sending something away. The paper is usually folded three times in total. Aside from speaking and doing, another factor sometimes comes into play in Appalachian folk magic: time and place.

THERE'S A TIME AND PLACE FOR EVERYTHING

We previously went over how the mountaineers figured from the Word that there's a time for just about everything, whether it's planting corn or going to the dentist. This practice of following the signs was adhered to by just about everyone. Root doctors and folk healers in Appalachia followed a particular system of timing, to aim the work just right for the highest outcome.

Appalachian folklore ascribes special gifts of healing and foresight to those born on certain days, such as March 11, January 1, Good Friday, February 14, Christmas Day or Eve, and Pentecost, among other "high days." Particular formulas are done only at certain times according to lore or if it is to include ingredients gathered at a certain time, such as the first rain collected in April or something to be performed when the rooster crows in the morning. This includes the "teller days," when people would track the weather on the Twelve Days of Christmas to predict the weather for each month of the coming year, with Day 1 for January, Day 2 for February, etc.

Time was even followed down to the hands of the clock. If you're dispelling something, do it as the big hand of the clock is going down, between12:01 and 5:59. If you are attracting something, work as the hand moves up, between 6:31 and 11:59. Midnight, however, was good for any work needing to be done. This is also applied to sunrise and sunset. Other times, certain times of the clock are ascribed to be good for luck, love, and so forth. For example, 6:00 a.m. or p.m. is good for calling a lover home; 11:00 a.m. or p.m. is good for cleansing.

For many works, like jar or bottle spells, they are repeated until results manifest. Some workings can take days to show results, while others can take a year or more. This is why it is called work: you have to keep working it, keep praying over it, keep feeding it to give it power and momentum. Some cures or curses will need to be done continuously over a period of time because of this, either for a number of consecutive days or a number of times on a number of consecutive days of the week. For example, cures are often done every Sunday for three consecutive Sundays.

We've spoken a few times about the importance of place, so I wanted to meet those loose ends here. A lot of value is placed in the land we work on, so much so that I've covered this ground over and over again. I welcomed you with the lay of the land, the terrain, and the weather to bring you into it, I advised you to connect with and learn about the animals, and I showed how our ancestors' lives were largely influenced and shaped by the land they worked and lived on. Based on what you've gathered through these pages, it should be evident that some places, often out of the way and rarely found, are believed to hold special powers. We'll begin with the church.

In Appalachia, religion is very important and is at the center of the home and family. The church and portions of the service held power for the conjure folk in these hills: stuff a handkerchief up your sleeve during church communion on Easter Sunday. As you take communion with that same hand, the handkerchief is indirectly imbued with powers of healing and protection. The same power can be derived by laying an open handkerchief on your lap during the Easter or Christmas sermon. Dirt collected from the churchyard at noon, right when the hand of the clock begins its descent, is powerful for protection from evil spirits, witchcraft, and theft. Dust from inside a church was also added to teas to heal a multitude of complaints.

Paired with this were the places prescribed by folklore and tradition to hold special power. These were graveyards, a crossroads, a crooked tree, or the place where a creek parts into two. Other times these places were obscure and rare, such as a lightning-struck tree standing in grave-yard, or a patch of grass where a lamb has recently laid. Lightning-struck trees bring misfortune and cursing, although healing is magnetized by the spirits of the dead when paid for with coins and whiskey; and the place where a lamb or deer has rested, which we call "the Lord's Rest," is collected on Sundays for powders to bring peace in the home, a salve to bring rest for those who are ill, and in charms to protect children.

Other types of places and times aren't physical at all; they are states of an environment or situation. For example, some remedies or formulas can only be administered as long as the person it is for has no knowledge of it. Other times the success of a formula done alone is highly based on the secrecy of it, especially in works of cursing or crossing. Folklore says if you are seen doing the work, then the work is useless and will need to be done again. This same theory applies to making sachets and samuels. If someone watches you do the work, they will steal the power from it.

Now that you know of the working space, when and where certain formulas are performed, and where works are often disposed of or hidden, we can put this knowledge to use. Let's now turn to some of the herbs and ingredients we use.

WHAT MAKES A ROOT?

Roots, tobies, charms, and brews are composed of ingredients believed to hold power. This power is ascribed to them by observation of nature, the doctrine of signatures (the belief that God marked each thing with a clue of its metaphysical purpose), and folklore that has survived in Appalachia from its roots.

Waters and Spirits

The mountains are scattered with creeks, fens, rivers, and lakes that continue to hold the magical qualities ascribed to them by the European immigrants, African slaves, and native peoples. In Appalachia, these have turned into an array of different waters used in remedies and charms. We also use spirits such as moonshine, whiskey, and tequila.

Other waters are man-made by mixing herbs with certain waters or putting water into certain environments and circumstances. Known in folklore as Adam's ale, water is employed by sprinkling it, spitting it, bathing in it, ingesting it, and anointing the body with the waters or spirits. Following are a few different waters employed in Appalachia.

RAINWATER

Rainwater should be collected in a white porcelain bowl held up to the sky. It cannot touch the ground and still be considered rainwater. Rainwater is used for healing skin diseases or afflictions and is used in teas for physical or spiritual ailments. The first rain in May is very beneficial for all kinds of healing as well as protection, while the first rain caught in April is good for attracting love. Because of the saying, "April showers bring May flowers," I have named this type of water April Showers.

Rainwater caught in a cobalt blue glass is drunk for toothache, and water caught on Maundy Thursday or Easter Sunday is great for healing, protection, and cleansing. The Irish would sprinkle it on the backs of livestock thought to be witched. Rainwater collected during a thunderstorm after the first flash of lightning can be added to brews or works to add strength to the qualities of the herbs.

CREEK AND RIVER WATER

Also utilized in healing, creek and river water is best collected either with the tide or against the tide (based on the remedy or formula) and used as a base for teas and washes. It is also used for cleansing or removing roots from a person, but in order for it to retain this spirit of cleansing it has to be free-flowing and "alive," which means you cannot store it for this purpose.

OCEAN WATER

I spoke previously about the healing power of ocean water. It can also be used for fertility. A preacher presents to the would-be mother ocean water in a mason jar steeped with a handful of chickpeas. From the jar she will take a bit and rub it over her navel and on the big toe of each foot while saying the Lord's Prayer and wearing a child's bonnet around her neck.

DEW

A famous ingredient in folk magic across the world, dew has powerful properties, as it is the earth's "sweat" after a hot day. Wash your face with the morning dew before sunrise on the first of May for help with skin ailments such as rashes, or wash your chest and seat with the dew to treat depression (or "falling back," as Nana calls it).

Women who wish to gain the affections of a certain love wash their face, breast, and bits with the dew while saying the person's name; and those women who wish to be heavy with child that year will roll around in the dew in the light of the full moon.

Depending on formulas and remedies as well as their purpose, dew is collected from specific places such as the oldest grave's headstone, the arms of a wooden cross, or the grass itself by running the hand to get it or wiping it up with a white handkerchief. Dew is also connected to a belief in an old folk illness called "dew poisoning"; folks believed that dew could cause sores on the bottoms of the feet if you went barefooted.

STUMP WATER

Also called spunk water due to its sometimes funky smell, stump water is ascribed power because it has never touched the earth and therefore still holds the virtues of the volt of heaven. Just any water from a stump won't do, though, according to the few sources of Appalachian folklore.

It has to be collected on a full moon while the moon is reflecting in the water, with a silver ladle dipped straight down into it. You must walk backward to the stump, and you have to be silent from the moment you leave your abode until you return. I have an old ladle made of silver that I acquired for just this purpose. Before I had the ladle, I could only make use of the water while present at the stump, still walking backward in silence to make it there.

Stump water and its virtues come from the Cherokee. In "The Swimmer Manuscript" by James Mooney, an informant notes that a Cherokee elder named Spencer Bird used water scooped from a stump for healing. With water being the primary tool this elder used, stump water was held in high regard in his practice and by the Cherokee tribe as a whole. As the water has never touched the ground, it continued to hold the blessings of heaven and was called "flying water."

Tobacco Juice

Used in multiple cross-cultural traditions of folk magic and medicine, tobacco juice makes a good medicine for bug bites, rashes, wounds, and infected places. The Cherokee and Delaware Indians would chew tobacco and spit the juice on snakebites, dog bites, beestings, and cuts. If you feel you'd rather not chew the tobacco and spit the juice, add three parts cut tobacco to one part water to an 8-ounce mason jar and mash it around with a thick stick or a pestle. Let it sit for three days, strain, and add two pinches of salt to preserve.

Easter Water

Easter water is holy water that's been acquired from the church (no matter the denomination) after the Easter Sunday sermon, or any rainwater that's caught on Easter, should it rain that day. Easter water is used in all forms of healing and protection, and also in divination.

Good Water

Good water is any kind of natural, living water collected on Good Friday. It holds amazing power in healing and dispelling disease or other ailments. However, no other water must be used on that day—no dishes or clothes should be washed, or they will break or have stains that will never come out. European folklore blames this on a tale that while going to Calvary, Christ was assaulted by a woman who threw dirty dishwater on him.

Moonshine

Originating through the Scots-Irish who brought it to Appalachia in the 1800s, moonshine was known as *uisce beatha*, (*ish-ka bah-ha*) which is Gaelic for "water of life." Throughout the stories told in these hills, it has been ascribed a wide array of qualities. Everyone knows the famous image of moonshiners making their "dew" in the graveyards. Moonshine made in a graveyard would have the attributes of spiritual communication and protection. Its value was doubled because it was far easier to carry out on wagon than cornhusks were. Because of its usually high proof, it is good for cleansing and protecting as well as facilitating other properties for good luck and love. Sprinkle some on the crown of your head and wipe it on the back of your neck when going into a graveyard for protection from haints. It's also good for colds and congestion.

Whiskey

Whiskey was always one of my mother's go-to remedies for a cold, aided by other ingredients to make a hot toddy. For diarrhea, a tablespoon of whiskey was carefully lit until the flame went out and it cooled. This "burnt whiskey" was taken two or three times a day. Besides its medicinal value, it also makes a good hand wash for cleansing, good luck, and love. It is also a good offering to be left for the spirits, human or otherwise. If it is to be used as an offering, don't give any alcohol to those who had problems with drinking or who died because of complications related to alcohol. I don't recommend using the cinnamon whiskey, either—it's sticky on the hands.

Tar Water

Made by steeping pine tar in water for a few days and straining off the excess tar, tar water is used for cleansing, purging homes of haints, and removing crossings or curses.

Dirts, Dusts, and Minerals

The use of dirts and dusts in Appalachian folk magic and other American traditions can be traced back to a number of cultures and people, namely the Scottish, Irish, British, Germans, Africans, and native tribes. Dirt contains the spiritual essence or the root of a particular place and, like water, can be used for a multitude of purposes. Charms such as prayer cloths, pokes, and bottles of water can be buried in certain places to absorb some of that spiritual power.

Mud was often applied to wounds, bug bites, and snakebites. Dirt from a church or courthouse was carried by people who wanted to avoid the law. And snake heads were powdered and discretely planted in a person's well to "poison" them. The use of dirts and dusts digressed into using homemade powders of flour or cornmeal and different minerals such as sulfur and gunpowder. Dirts are sprinkled into the shoes or on the garments of the person it is intended for, sprinkled where they will walk over it, scattered around the home to act as a guard or for another purpose, and sometimes added to teas by placing it in a cotton bag and soaking it in the boiling brew.

Graveyard Dirt

Dirt from a graveyard is taken either from a particular grave or a corner of the cemetery itself. From a grave, the dirt is mostly used to employ the spirit of that grave for the work at hand, but sometimes it's simply "bought" or "replaced." Information from oral and written lore in Appalachia recommends its use in healing remedies and other charms including love, gambling, protection, and cursing. One such example was for a woman to miscarry a child she did not want. She would go to the oldest grave or a new grave in a cemetery and eat a handful of the grass growing there. Then she would wait until the sun moved and the shadow of the headstone fell on her stomach. Now remember, this was before there was ready access to qualified doctors, so they could either go the dangerous route of aborting the child themselves with poisons and abuse or go with the old superstitions.

CHURCHYARD DIRT

Used in remedies for toothache, wounds, and general sickness, the dirt taken from the grounds of a church is also carried for protection against witchcraft and enemies, protection from the law, healing charms, and love work. Sometimes, "liver-grown" children were taken to the church to have the sides of their body rubbed against the walls on either side of the altar. Other times, dust from the floorboards of the church would be baked in bread or mixed with a glass of milk to treat sickness and bodily afflictions. Church dirt is best collected on a Sunday, and its power is often increased by collecting the dirt from seven or seventy-seven churches and mixing them together.

BANK OR MINE DIRT

The transition from using the dirt of a coal mine to that from a bank likely started when people began storing their money in banks instead of the mattress. Before that, the coal mine was a prized symbol of wealth for the people of Appalachia, and many superstitions arose around it to protect the mine from collapsing due to its strong economic influence. Women weren't allowed inside the mine at all, and no one was to whistle in its vicinity for fear of rousing evil spirits who may bring a collapse and take lives. This dirt was often carried in a sachet for good luck, money, and success in business dealings. It can be sprinkled in your shoes or even brewed into a tea to wash the hands for gambling. Charms for money can also be buried at a bank for three days to further bless it with the root of that land.

RAILROAD DIRT

Because the railroad symbolizes coming and going, its dirt is used to send people away or bring them home, or it can be added to charms for safe travel. For this, the dirt would have to come from a railroad that is still in use, whereas the soil from an abandoned railroad, I have found, makes good for keeping people, especially lovers, at home.

DIRT FROM A RABBIT'S DEN

Note: If you acquire dirt from a rabbit's den, please do not disturb any kittens that may be in the hole! Dirt from their den can be used in charms to ease depression, to improve fertility, and to encourage safe childbirth. To make a charm for safe childbirth, assemble the dust from a church, den dirt, and tobacco into a pouch for the woman to carry. At the time of birth she should undo the knots of the strings and pour the contents into the father's shoes, which she will then wear during delivery.

CROSSROADS

The crossroads are seen as a place of power, of coming and going, of calling and leaving. Crossroads dirt should be paid for with three of the shiniest dimes you can find. It can be used for removing obstacles from your path, calling a lover home, encouraging good luck, and just about anything that entails acquiring or removing something, whether spiritual or material.

Cow Droop

As cows walk on the grassy hills, their footsteps create an indention in the hillside. Dirt from these worn paths can be carried to aid depression and the fits, protect from witchcraft, and treat worms in man or beast, cure fevers, and more. It is best collected before dawn and preferably when neither the sun nor the moon is in the sky. Collect three thimblefuls and place in a bag around the neck for protection from conjure and depression. For worms, a tea is stewed from a cup of the dirt and consumed over the course of three days.

Police Station Dirt

Primarily used in either drawing the law to a person or keeping it away, this dirt is useful for situations that need charms to keep the law away. I will also use it to have someone tracked down and arrested.

Courthouse Dirt

Courthouse dirt is best used in works for positive outcomes in court. Moss from any steps or statuary on the grounds can also be used, as well as splinters of wood from the seats of the courtroom. Of course, getting a splinter today would be difficult; many courthouses will have you empty your pockets upon entering, and you may have to walk through a metal detector. I'd stick with gathering dirt with a spoon; it's a bit crazy looking, but way less threatening.

Flint

Used in solid form, flint provides protection in a number of cases. It is put in the fireplace to keep hawks from getting any of the chickens, it is hung up on a found cord in a barn to protect the cows from drying up, and it's hung from a tree on the property to protect from unwanted visitors. (If you haven't noticed, we don't like surprise visits much.)

RED CLAY

Often called redding, red clay is used much the same as red brick dust in the Deep South. It's sometimes added to water to make a pigment for wool and clothes, and it can be paired with new salt and black pepper and sprinkled in the shoes for protection from witchcraft and bad luck. Red clay is also used in remedies for bug bites, rashes, and shingles.

ANIMAL EXCREMENT

Whether dried or fresh, excrement from certain animals has been used in all parts of the world—and it's no different in Appalachia. The excrement is often given the same or similar attributes of power as the animal who made it. We've seen how the bulk strength of the bull is transferred to his manure, which is bandaged to the arm or limb to effect a cure. Goat manure is also dried, powdered, and rubbed on the backs of other livestock to protect them from bewitchment.

SULFUR

Often considered both a healing remedy and a cursed thing, water from a sulfur spring was a cure-all for just about anything. But sulfur could also work against someone—when walked over, it was a curse. For this trick, sulfur powder is mixed with local soil and black pepper so it is not noticeable.

COPPER

Belief in copper's healing properties is held worldwide, and it is still held strongly in Appalachia. Nana used to wear a bracelet with a copper cross for arthritis, and others still wear a bracelet of simple copper wire, turned three times to act as a protection against illness and even venereal disease. Water that is steeped with pennies can be used for arthritis and pains, since some families couldn't spare one twist of wire because it was going to be sold for extra money for the rest of the month.

Silver

Alas, the cliché of silver bullets still lingers. In many works on Appalachian and Ozark superstition, stories are told of shooting silver bullets at the moon while cursing God to become a witch. Other times the bullets (sometimes simple pellets pounded out of quarters back in the day) were used in works to find out and kill the witch inflicting harm on a family. Some cures also recommend the use of silver in easing ailments and healing sickness, as silver was believed to be an effectual method against these, along with a belief that it could cure infection.

Gold

Gold is considered the metal of God. The old-timers saw it as being seven times better at healing than copper. Gold chain necklaces could be worn to act the same as the copper twists in protecting against disease but also against evil spirits, as it was one of the gifts presented to the Christ child. Gold is also worn as a protection against the evil eye and misfortune.

Gunpowder

Add gunpowder to a work to give it strength and a good "shot." It is often employed in works of good luck, cursing, and protection. Gunpowder was also used in many remedies, often in the form of teas, but this isn't recommended.

Powders

Special powders can also be made by grinding herbs with salt and cornmeal. I personally find that adding salt to a mortar helps the grinding process. First get the herbs to a fine powder with the salt, and then add the mixture to an equal part of cornmeal. Bless the powder by praying over a glass of water and sprinkling the water into the powder and mixing it into clumps. Then allow it to dry. Place it in the center of three candles set in a triangle and pray the Lord's Prayer followed by your prayers for the powder's use. Do this three times a day (sunrise, noon, and sunset) for three days, and the powder is ready.

The powder is employed the same as dirt: in places it will be crossed over, applied to the body directly, or scattered around the home to bring money or success. One famous method is to grind eggshells and red bricks up into a powder with salt and cornmeal while praying Psalm 23. This is used to line the doors, windows, and boundaries of the property for protection. An old love powder was to get heart-shaped leaves, dry and powder them with orange hard candy and sugar. This was dusted on the potential lover's clothes without them knowing, usually the back of the collar or back of the arm.

HERBS AND CURIOS

Certain herbs and curios repeatedly find their way into charms and tricks throughout American folk magic. Appalachia was no exception here. As we've seen throughout this book, different herbs and animal parts or byproducts had to be acquired in a certain way or at a certain time to have any significant value. Many books have been written on this, but I will only speak of their Appalachian uses here.

Herbs

The following herbs are pretty easy to find in Appalachia, and are frequently used in all kinds of different workings.

BLOODROOT

Prized as a remedy for bleeding and sore wounds, the whole root of bloodroot was sometimes strung into a necklace to be worn to ward off nosebleeds. For bleeding charms, it should be harvested when the sign is in the feet. It is also good for situations involving family, love, and money.

Corn Silk and Root

Carried or used for love, employment, money, and good luck, corn silk is the Irish moss of Appalachia. It's made into a tea to help children who wet the bed and elders who can't retain their water. Pluck it from the corn before it is harvested while saying, "The hand of Mary plucked the hairs for all the nations." The fat roots at the base of the cornstalk are clipped off in fall and saved for teas used to cure bedwetting in children. Add corn root to workings against poverty and depression and for protection and physical strength.

Dandelion

Literally "lion's tooth," the whole root of the dandelion plant is used to exert your will on a situation or person. Besides being a good spring tonic and food, dandelion root can be carried to help with depression, soaked in warm water and rolled on a paining body part for relief, or carried for success in job interviews. I've heard the "milk" of the stem is also a good cure for warts.

Ginseng

Ginseng is one of the most beloved herbs in Appalachia for its culinary and medicinal uses, as well as its financial value. Some families harvest and sell it to help get by until the first of the month. The Cherokee say it is the chief of the plant people and was the one to decree that all plants will make a cure for any disease sent to afflict man. Because of this, ginseng is carried for good luck and success, much like High John the Conqueror root.

GOLDENROD

Goldenrod makes a good tonic for women's menstrual cramps and bloating. In Appalachia, the blooms are used for business, money, and court. To draw in money, sprinkle the tiny blooms in the four corners of the home while praying, beginning with the Lord's Prayer. For court, mix new salt with powdered goldenrod and sprinkle some as you go into the door of the courthouse. While in the courtroom, as secretly as you can, drop a pinch or so every time the judge says something—but make sure you're on the right side of justice.

GOLDENSEAL

Cherokee and European hunters carried goldenseal to ward off snakes—particularly the rattler. The root may also be carried for good luck, general health, and money, particularly if it is dug up with your left hand on a Friday during a full moon.

MAYAPPLE

The roots of mayapple are carried for luck in love and finances. Bind your hair and that of your lover's around the root while praying the Lord's Prayer, followed by your petition. Hide it beneath your mattress to encourage fidelity between you both.

PAWPAW

A native fruit-bearing tree in Appalachia, pawpaw has always been associated with witchcraft and the dead. Pawpaw roots can be carried to protect from haints, to lay a curse on someone, or to heal addictions by cutting the root; for the latter cause, measure each "dose" with half an empty eggshell. Three doses are measured, and a dose of root is made into a poultice with flour, salt, and water, which is applied to the upper right side of the abdomen until it dries. Don't mix it enough to create a dough, though—mix just enough to create a sticky putty.

Carry nine pawpaw seeds sewn tightly in a bag to warm you when you've walked over "something." If made and blessed right, it'll jump to warn you and also kill that work if it's for you.

Potato

Coming from the Irish healing tradition, the potato makes an appearance in Appalachian cures for warts, deep wounds, and charms for good luck. Carry one in your left pocket for luck or rub a half on a wart and bury it under the eaves of the house or barn. They can also be carved into dolls (we've also done the same with soap and coal in my family).

Putty Root

Putty root is the infamous root Adam and Eve sold for use in love workings. The Cherokee carried bits of it for good luck in games of chance and for love. You can carry putty root in a deerskin bag for good luck in hunting.

Trillium Root

Also known as Little John or Low John, trillium root was chewed the morning one had to go into court to gain favor with the judge. Harvest the roots in the spring on a Friday, and hang them up in a bundle to dry, to keep the law away. You'll need to feed them every month by dabbing whiskey on each stem while saying your prayers.

Trout Lily

Best picked in the spring while it is blooming, trout lilies were given (in my area) as courting charms. Carry the root to find the affections of your sweetheart or wash your face with the juices before meeting with them. The juices were also used as an eyewash for many afflictions.

WALNUT

The walnut tree finds its way into Appalachian folklore just as much as the willow. Grated and dusted walnut hulls are used for a brown to black dye for clothes, and the leaves are scattered about the house at sunset and left until morning, when they're swept out, to get rid of troublesome spirits. Walnuts are also used in cursing, protection, and uncrossing. Carry an unripe walnut in your pocket for rheumatism and arthritis. As it ripens and dries out, so will the aching.

YARROW

Yarrow's uses are varied but practically intact from European lore in Appalachia. It is used for cleansing, healing, and protection. For cleansing, take up one stalk that has ten blades. Pluck the tenth off and cast it away. Make the sign of the cross on the person's chest and back, rubbing it on the head and the bottoms of their feet. Then burn it, away from the home. Yarrow can also be used for love workings to gain the affections of another.

Curios

Other objects besides herbs are used in Appalachian workings as well. Here are a few of the most common ones.

COINS

Minted before 1964, silver dimes are worn around the ankle or neck to protect from conjurations, particularly those set on the ground for you to walk over. It is said the silver dime will turn black when you have walked over a trick, the reason being most powders for harm contained sulfur. I've been wearing the same dime for about five years now, and while it hasn't turned black due to something I have walked over, it has sometimes fallen off. To me, this is another way it shows me something's up. Bent coins are carried for luck, as are pennies found heads-up. Holed pennies are also worn for different purposes: a hole through Abraham's head treats headaches; a hole through the heart addresses heart issues and love; a hole in front of Abraham brings good luck, and a hole behind him protects from conjure. However, pennies for yourself cannot be holed by you or in your home; those must be done elsewhere by someone other than you, using a nail and hammer.

FEATHERS

The bird from which the feathers originate determines their use. Dove feathers can be added to a pillow to ward off nightmares; duck feathers are carried for good luck in money; feathers from a black hen that hasn't laid eggs yet is good for protection from conjure; and buzzard feathers hung above the doorway can avert illness. Again, a friendly reminder that it is against federal law in the United States to possess anything of a migratory or songbird under the Migratory Bird Treaty Act of 1918, which includes the possession of feathers, eggs, nests, and anything that is made or used by the bird.

LOCKS AND TIES

Often called personal concerns by the general magical community, locks and ties are any object that connects intimately to a person. Different ties have certain values based on the intimacy of that connection. For example, a picture of a person or their handwriting isn't as strong as a drop of their blood or a hair freshly plucked from their head. We've seen several examples throughout this book for how hair, unwashed garments, and nail clippings are used in Appalachian conjure.

RED FLANNEL

Red flannel is believed to carry special powers of good luck and protection from the evil eye.

STONES

Stones from particular places such as a churchyard, a graveyard, or a crossroads may be included in a sachet. A practice that spread from Pennsylvania down to Virginia was the "dar rootie" (a corruption of *der ruhkschtee*, German for "stone of stillness"). It was a stone that was placed on a fence post and left alone for a full moon cycle, after which it was helpful with insomnia, colicky babies, and pain and stress. Peepstones, also called hag stones, are rocks with natural holes in them that are carried for good luck and protection from the little folk.

TURKEY BONES

Turkey bones have a long history in Appalachia for enticing lust and romance in a partner. Hide a bone under your loved one's bed, bury it at their door, or slip it under the seat of their car. (Back in the day most men drove trucks, and women would slip a bone behind the driver's seat.)

Written Charms

Written charms consist of holy writ or folk verses copied on paper to be carried close to the skin, either tied to an afflicted limb for healing or in a pocket. Here are a couple of examples.

For pregnant women, the following may be written on paper and kept close to the skin for the duration of the pregnancy:

*

I.N.R.I.
+ *Jesus Mary Joseph* +

This charm provides protection, health, and blessings to the mother-to-be by the names of the blessed family who were sheltered, helped, and kept safe in the direst of circumstances.

The next charm is written and kept on a sick person to enact heal-ing or is burned on Christmas Eve and the ashes kept in the home for good luck throughout the next year. It consists of writing the names of the Three Kings who brought gifts to Jesus with the Star above them:

*

Gasper

Balthasar   *Melchior*

If the above is to be used for healing, place the written charm in a cloth bag and keep it as close to the skin as possible. If it is burned to bring good fortune to the home, the ashes are left in the back of the fireplace and are never to be cleaned out. To make sure they aren't removed unknowingly, surround the ashes with white stones to sep-arate them from the other ashes and simply clean around the stones for the year.

Jacks and Packets

In Appalachia, jacks, jack thumbs, jimmies, tobies, hands, sachets, roots, and sains are understood to generally mean the same thing, although a sain is particularly used for protection, blessing, and cleansing—and jimmies are for healing. These are charms containing different herbs or curios carried in order to work their magic. Folklore differs on how long they should be carried, and there are different methods for caring for them.

No one is allowed to see your "hand," and it should never touch the ground. Should this happen, it should be tossed out and another one made. If you are good at keeping things hidden, then you may be able to keep your sachet for a very long time and simply repair it when it begins to fall apart by patching it in more fabric and sewing it together again. One of my mother's bags for keeping the law away has been car-ried and repaired for a good eight years now and is close to retirement.

Other times the nonperishable contents can be transferred to a new "skin" and blessed again.

Different workers have their own way of creating a toby or packet. As I was taught, each item is simply placed on a square piece of fabric. The number of items varies based on region and family, but generally it is kept at odd numbers such as 1, 3, 5, 7, 9, or 13. I sometimes employ charms composed of one simple herb or curio, such as the necklace I wear now, which is a whole nutmeg wrapped and sewn in a scrap of flannel to avert toothache and cold.

Before being placed on the fabric, all the ingredients you plan to use are prayed over, spat upon, or rolled with the fingers in the palm of the hand while praying or cursing. The fabric is then bound around the items by bringing all the corners together and tying it with a red cord, knotted three times in the name of the Trinity. Leave about six inches of cord hanging off and clip the excess.

The charm now needs to be blessed, which also differs based on lore and people's regional practice. Sometimes, I will simply rub and breathe on it, praying silently. Other times, I will sprinkle it with holy water, baptize it with some 'shine, or leave it for the spirits to bless.

Following is an example of how you can "witch" your hand for the work. Lift the bag by the string and dip it into a glass of clean water quickly and invoke the Trinity:

> *In the name of God the Father, God the Son, and God*
> *the Holy Spirit, I baptize this sachet by my name for*
> *[state the intention of the charm].*

This is baptizing it with the water. Now it needs to be baptized by the fire.

Light a candle that has been anointed with oil blessed by reciting Psalm 23. Hold the hand up by the string and begin swinging it back and forth through the flame of the candle while praying to the spirits to bless the charm. Make sure to keep a consistent swing through the flame while praying so as not to burn the sachet or catch it on fire. Say your prayer three times:

> *In the name of the Father, the Son, and the Holy Ghost,*
> *[petition or prayer . . .]*

Once you're done blessing it by fire, smoke it with tobacco smoke and pour a bit of whiskey over it. Feed it with the same type of whiskey every week or month to keep it "alive." You've put a root or spirit in it, and you have to "remind" it with the whiskey of what its job is so it doesn't die.

To make a jack thumb or packet, get a square piece of paper you've torn from a brown paper bag. Place pinches of herb or root in the paper and fold it up. Bind it and bless it with the Lord's Prayer. Blow tobacco smoke on it three times and finish by doing so in the name of the Trinity. Feed this with a drop of whiskey. When folded, it should be about the same length and width as your thumb. After this, I will leave the sachet or packet for the spirits to bless for three days, during which I pray the same petitions over them in the morning, at noon, and at night.

Candle Magic

Candles and oil lamps are another thing in Appalachia surrounded by superstition. They were often used in home remedies and even in determining when a person would die. A tapered candle was sat in a holder next to the bed of someone sick, especially when the predicament seemed hopeless. The timing of death could be seen when the candle made a "winding sheet" in the direction of the ill—tears of wax that have run down the side in the same place over and over again, forming a large protrusion from the candle. Another omen of death was the coffin handle—when the wick curls in on itself, creating a complete loop.

Three candles should never be sat in a row and lit or it will bring death; an oil lamp should never be allowed to run dry or it will invite misfortune. Candles and lamps are used as offerings to the spirits one is working with and to send the prayer out. A candle burned at a wake was sometimes rubbed on the skin for pains or wounds, and the remains of any candle burned during the last Christmas dinner is rubbed on a bad bruise for three days—usually Wednesday, Thursday, and Friday. However, my Mamaw Morgan never bothered with that. She'd just head up a sewing needle, prick it, and draw the blood out from it.

The methods for using candles and lamps are somewhat plain and not very elaborate in Appalachian folk magic. Taper candles are the most commonly used, aside from glass-encased vigil candles, which are simply dressed with olive oil on the top of the wax while praying. Other times, I will tear strips of cotton cloth and write my prayer on the fabric. I then tie the cloth around the glass candle at the bottom.

With a taper candle, the person's name is carved into the side or three simple X's are marked into it. To anoint a candle, rub your hands with olive oil while praying and then rub the candle with the oil. Sometimes the candle is stuck with nine pins or needles if the work is a curse. Prior, I also roll the candle away from me if I'm sending something away or toward me to draw something.

The placement of the candle when it's ready to burn is determined by the work. Sometimes more than one candle is called for, with the usual number being three. Color isn't really specified, as most candles back then were simply white or off-white. In works of healing, I will place the person's photo down, on the back of which I have written the petition, and surround it with four candles, creating a quincunx to add power to the work by symbolically calling up the crossroads to send a disease or illness away. Oftentimes, I will simply use three candles set in a triangle to represent the Holy Trinity.

Now for oil lamps, you'll just need to wash out the basin of the lamp with saltwater and then fill it with the herbs you'll be using, along with any other curios. The best thing about oil lamps is that the flame is away from the ingredients and is fed only by the oil infused with the prayers of the herbs. This way, the actual ingredients do not perish right away, and the lamp can be used for months or years. Once the basin is filled with the oil and herbs, make the sign of the cross over it and whisper your prayer into the vessel and blow three breaths into the basin.

Place the top on, light the wick while saying your prayer again, and affix the glass chimney. Make sure the flame isn't turned on too high, as it can be dangerous; just make sure the flame is about the size produced by a modern lighter. The lamp can be burned every day from sunrise to sunset or by the hands of the clock. Make sure to say your prayer again as you light it, but don't leave it burning unattended, and don't let the oil burn all the way up. Lamps are usually for long-term works such as good health, protection, help in dealing with diseases, and as a simple offering to the spirits. To strengthen the work, you can get a clothespin and attach your prayer paper to the wick inside the basin, so the roots pass through it to the flame.

Candles and lamps are sometimes placed in bowls or buckets and surrounded with water or other offerings to the spirits, such as fruits, herbs, foods, and candies. Just make sure the items aren't flammable, and don't position them close to the flame, as it deconstructs the candle. In the case of a lamp, don't let it touch the chimney. Other times, the candle or lamp can be placed on a closed Bible. We've seen how the Bible is infused by the minds of believers and nonbelievers alike with power and importance. I wouldn't recommend setting it on an open Bible, however, as the curve of the pages could make it a possible fire hazard.

Bottles, Jars, and Cans

The use of certain bottles and tin cans in American folk magic has been documented by such people as Vance Randolph, Harry Hyatt, and other folklorists across the country, as well as construction workers, electricians, and gravediggers who sometimes find them buried at doorways, under fireplaces, and hidden in walls. Their use reaches back to the beliefs of ancient Egypt, where bottles and vessels could apparently capture souls and spirits.

This belief, along with the power attributed to the color "haint blue," traveled northward into Europe and southward into Africa, simultaneously carrying the seeds that would soon come full circle in European immigration and the slave trade to rest in the New World, resulting in the infamous southern decoration we know as the bottle tree. The belief was that the spirits of demons and haints who wander around at night would be lured by the color of the bottles and get trapped into them, only to vaporize when the sun rose. According to Nana, it didn't get rid of them or kill them, though; it only held them in the bottle until daybreak, which is the time they are required to fade back into their lonesome realms. Considering some haints are simply human beings lost between worlds due to trauma and violent deaths, I took comfort that they didn't die a second time. Simply put in a cage for the night, per se.

One of my grandmothers had one in her yard. It was a cherry tree that parted at the soil into two trees, one of which had died off and no longer came to leaf. It was on that side that she hung her cobalt blue, red, and green bottles. Sadly, the tree had to be cut down. She has since had a two-by-four of wood planted as a pole, with metal protrusions sticking out to adorn with the bottles. Her mother never relied on the bottle tree, though: the front porch to her mountain trailer had to have held thirty or more wind chimes to scare the haints away.

Bottles were also used for divination and charms throughout Ireland and Scotland and came to root in the Southern Uplands, as the inside of a bottle is a controlled environment, one the folk witch creates inside with ingredients, ties, and whispers. One example of bottle work was to "stop someone up": Wake in the morning and without speaking, collect your urine in a bottle. Take some tie or link to them, whether it's hair, nails, or a photo, and place it in the bottle. Continue in silence and bury the bottle upside down under a tree. This is said to "stop them up" so they cannot urinate, leading to death. Appalachian and Ozark folklore record this being used to kill a person if they were indeed the witch who had inflicted harm upon the family. We also have a handful of stories about Biddy Early, an Irish witch who was gifted a magic bottle in which she could see the fated outcomes of treatments and whether or not her assistance would help those that came to her. Further, there's more bottle lore about magic bottles containing little men who would come out and do the bidding of the bottle's owner.

Another example is the witch bottle. Found in various cultures, the witch bottle was primarily used as a protective charm against being witched. They often contain sharp objects such as nails, pins, needles, or broken glass, and urine and ties to those under its protection. In Appalachian folk magic, they are buried at doorsteps, sat in windowsills, concealed in walls, and hidden in chimneys or attics.

A bottle recipe I have used for years is as follows: Place your urine, nails, and hair into the bottle. If the bottle is for a whole household, add beet juice and have each member of the family spit into the bottle. The bottle is best placed away from the family, as far as reasonable, such as the property lines. Spirits and charms deployed against you will take the shortest path to what it thinks is you, which is the reason behind the witching bottle: it's a decoy.

Next, nine of each or a combination of nails, pins, and needles are placed into the bottle. A bundle of red string, knotted tightly, may also be jammed into the bottle to further entrap curses, spirits, or general negativity set out for you. Once the bottle is capped and shut tight, coat it with a layer of moist red clay. Then bake it in a firepit by hold-ing it in the flames held aloft by an iron shovel. While it heats up the contents and the mud dries, recite the full chapter of Psalm 59.

Syrup jars were also used to sweeten situations or people, be it a mean boss or feuding lovers. On a Friday, as the hand of the clock moves up, fill a jar with syrup, sugar, and four tablespoons of water along with your petition and a tie to the person. Fill it while saying your prayers for the person to sweeten up to you, for honey to coat their tongue when speaking your name, and for the scent of roses to surround your presence. When done, cap the jar tight and shake it while praying some more. Continue working the jar like this every day at the same time until the situation improves. These kinds of work I don't get rid of. I work it as needed after it has manifested, usually when the work begins to slip and needs a little push. I'll also put it on the stovetop to get things to "move smoothly." Not too hot, though—just warm enough that the contents move smoothly.

Tin cans are sometimes used instead of bottles, as they were sim-ply what was at hand. One example of a charm to bring back a lover uses a tin can: Take a red onion and cut a cross-like incision into it, one vertical and one horizontal. Inside the cut place a bit of your first morning's urine, along with a strip of your love's dirty garments and a name paper or photo of them. Sit the onion in a tin can upright and pour whiskey over it in the name of the Father, the Son, and the Holy Ghost to bring your love home to you. Place the lid over the can and set it under the bed on their side. Each night for nine nights, toss a pinch of salt in while calling out their name and telling them to return to you.

Another way to use a tin can is for removing tricks or curses: pour a half-cup of whiskey and a half-cup of vinegar into a tin can. Place a white cloth bundle of new blessed salt no bigger than the width of three fingers in the can. Set the contents under the bed and have the cursed sleep over it until the whiskey and vinegar have fully evaporated from both can and bundle. Once the liquid is gone and the bundle is fully dry, rub the bundle three times from head to toe. Once this is done, wait for the following Sunday. On Sunday before sunrise, without speaking to anyone, place the bundle in the mouth and go outside, where you'll draw a circle in the dirt with a cross in it. The cross shouldn't reach the edges of the circle. While holding the bitter dickens in your mouth, face east and watch the sun rise. When the rooster crows, spit the bundle out onto the cross, spit on it three times, and bury it. Walk away and do not look back.

Knots

In Ireland and the British Isles, knotted cords and rope were sold to sailors, each knot installed with a gust of wind that was released when a knot was untied. And throughout Europe, a knotted cord called the witch's ladder was used to hold magical power. In Appalachia this same practice has been preserved, especially in folk remedies, as we've seen in the stopping of blood, the easing of fevers, and the curing of chills.

In most of Europe, there was a belief in faeries coming in the night and knotting your hair into matted links. This is often regarded as a sign of being cursed. In Appalachia, its meaning depends on the family: either you just slept like a rock, or you've been ridden by a haint. Knots are also subject to superstition. None of my grandmothers would knit, crochet, or sew during Old Christmas because they believed to do so would jinx their crafts for the next year: thread would knot, the knitters would miss loops, and the chains wouldn't come straight no matter what you did.

Placing a certain number of knots in a person's hair was believed to either drive them mad or straight out of town, while tying a knot in the corner of an apron proved good for many things, such as shooing an owl away (and with it omens of death). In Appalachia and the Ozarks, no knots were tied to take a man's aim at shooting a gun; instead, the strings of the apron were simply crossed to take the man's aim, to get strangers to go on their way, and to avert bad luck at the mention of ill fortune.[8]

Knots were created to bind, force, and encourage change in some way, whether that was calling a lover home, or keeping the law away, or averting evil spirits. There's a Bradford pear tree in my front yard that has handkerchiefs tied in knots on it for keeping troublesome people and haints away. Sometimes strands of horse or cow hair were tied in knots to protect them from bewitchment.

Numbers are frequently recommended when making knots for a certain work. To keep the law away, drag a red string between the lips of every person in the home, dust it with dirt taken from the doorstep or front yard, and tie five knots in it while commanding law enforcement to stay away. I often command this by saying,

> *In the name of the King of Kings, by the voice that cast Adam from the Garden and called Moses from the Mountain, may all people of the law and state stay far from my property and leave us be.*

You can say something along those lines as you tie each knot; afterward, hang the string above the front door. To be less noticeable, fasten it with some tape to the top of the doorframe where it meets the wall. The number five in this formula is obvious as a mathematical quincunx, taking into account the number of points at a crossroads.

Sometimes, numbers such as three and seven are used, or the number of knots should be the age of the person, the number of chills they've had, or the number of letters in their name. For inflammation in any part of the body, take a black ribbon that came from the person

---

[8] Randolph, Vance. *Ozarks Superstitions*. New York: Columbia University Press, 1947.

and tie a knot for each letter of their name. Soak it in whiskey for three days, and when you take it back up, bless it by the Trinity by making a cross sign over it three times, calling out the name of the person and the names of their father and mother. Leave it somewhere safe to dry out and remain.

Doll Babies

The last and possibly the most complex way of working roots and trying prayers is with doll babies and nannies, elsewhere known at poppets or voodoo dolls. They are employed for many reasons, some of which may seem morally questionable. However, aside from the sacrifice of Christ and his rebuking of the Old Testament laws, they were still followed, and many today still believe in "an eye for an eye, and a tooth for a tooth" instead of natural karma or turning the other cheek. As I mentioned before, it must be justified. Before any kind of curse work, I will pray Psalm 7:1–5 to remind myself that if my hand has tipped the scale, it's just that it fall on me:

> *O Lord my God, in thee do I put my trust: save me from all them that persecute me, and deliver me:*

> *Lest he tear my soul like a lion, rending it in pieces, while there is none to deliver.*

> *O Lord my God, If I have done this; if there be iniquity in my hands;*

> *If I have rewarded evil unto him that was at peace with me; (yea, I have delivered him that without cause is mine enemy:)*

> *Let the enemy persecute my soul, and take it; yea, let him tread down my life upon the earth, and lay mine honour in the dust. Selah.*

As with any culture or people, dolls were made mostly for children to play with, but some grown-ups also played with them to enact revenge, to bring people home or make them leave, or to bring healing or sickness to a person. The materials used to make dolls in Appalachia were extremely varied and were subject to the times. During the Great Depression, they were often made with hollowed cucumbers and sticks speared into a couple of potatoes. There wasn't a lot to be done once chores were taken care of, so a lot of time was spent creating clothes for the dolls. Go into any antique store today and look at the beautiful craftsmanship of the primitive dolls that may be there, the fabric crafted neatly into a human form and dressed with fabrics reminiscent of a christening gown or old tablecloth.

Mamaw had a doll that wore an enchanting green dress that always sat on her dresser next to a bunch of thimbles. Whether she made that one herself I have no clue of, but she did show me how to make dolls from a corncob once.

First and foremost, you need to understand that doll babies can be dangerous and can have unexpected effects. It's important to care for the doll regularly and never abandon it. I've experienced dolls moving on their own, among other phenomena, when they aren't treated properly.

One time I made a doll that I planned to use, but upon finishing it I no longer had need for it. So I left it to gather dust. The poor thing didn't even have a name. The only thing I can figure is my anger that was imbued in the doll through its creation may have played a factor. I woke up one night and saw that the doll was on my dresser, standing straight up on its own. Whether it was a dream or not I can't be certain, because I fell back asleep and only remember catching a glimpse of the booger. The next morning, I burned it. My hypothesis is that if you do not name the doll within a certain period, it may take on its own spirit and name itself!

Doll babies can also be dangerous if they are made wrong or are used in the wrong way. I had one person come to me about a year or so ago about a doll she made twenty-plus years ago from the dirty underwear and hair of a man she loved at the time. In the working, she said for him to love her forever and always want to be with her. Twenty-five years later, at least according to the last time we spoke, the man was still obsessed with her—waiting outside her work, coming to her house, and other forms of harassment—regardless of restraining orders. The doll had been buried for the working and in twenty years had disintegrated into nothing. All I could do was to advise her to do a candle work to reverse it.

Be mindful of how powerful these dolls and fetishes can be. Oftentimes, they're more powerful if you're ignorant about them. The ways of the universe, huh?

When working with doll babies, it's best to give the doll the same identity and essence of the person whose image it is made in. This can be done with a photo, a rag or napkin with their blood on it, nail clippings, a lock of hair, or an unwashed garment. The locks can be tied to the torso, stuffed into the head, or placed in the doll with the other stuffing. I prefer to place the item either in the head or the heart, the primary places of identity and awareness. If it is a shirt or some other garment, I use that to make the body of the doll.

The most widely known doll in Appalachia is the apple head doll. Often made for children, they were dressed as old people since the apple head wrinkles naturally, and each one takes on its own personality. These dolls were common primarily because just about every family had a couple of apple trees growing somewhere around the bend.

To make an apple head doll, start by peeling the skin off an apple. Once the skin is off, take your thumbnail and press in where the eyes should be. Below them, in the middle, press down vertically two times to make the sides of the nose, and then connect them at the bottom with one horizontal press to make the bottom of the nose. Then press to form the indention that will become the mouth when it dries, just about a centimeter below the bottom of the nose. Below that, make another indentation to form the upper potion of the chin beneath the lips.

You can also carve out a bit of the cheeks to make the cheekbones more prominent or make creases in the forehead in an attempt to direct the wrinkles during the drying process. Core a bit of the top out and save the "cap." You'll fill it with herbs, dirts, and personal concerns. Dip the apple head in lemon juice, submerging it entirely, and spear it with a stick through the core. Take another stick and tie it to the end of a strong cord, and then take the other end of the cord and thread it through the head so it sits at the end of the cord, supported by the stick. Set it aside to dry for about a week. The lemon juice affects the final result: use it for a lighter skin tone or don't use it for a darker or black tone.

For the doll body, get two pieces of thick, malleable wire—one 24 inches long and the other 4 to 5 inches long. Fold the longer piece of wire in half, forming a loop at one end. This is where the head will go. Take the shorter piece of wire and lay it across the looped wire to make the arms. Make sure there's about 4 inches of wire for the neck and head, because once the head is placed on, the end of the loop will be cut off and the wire turned down the back of the head to secure it.

Fasten the crossed wires with some string or tape so they will hold in that form. Then wrap strips of cloth around the intersection of the wires and around each limb, keeping the fabric as flat as you can. When you get to the end of one limb, fold the tip of the wire over on top of the fabric to keep it from slipping off. After you fold it, wrap backward to the torso. Keep doing this with every limb. If the loop is at the top, then you should have two separate wires sticking downward for the legs. Wrap them together with fabric, starting from the torso, as explained above, until you get a third of the way down, at which point you can separate them to form the individual legs, and wrap each leg as you did the arms.

It's best to dress the frame before placing the head on the doll. If you're not sure how to create good clothes for it, there are tutorials online that will help. Other times the doll can be wrapped with more fabric around the legs and arms to act as clothes. I usually just cut out cloth shaped for the arms and body and sew them together around the frame, but since the frame is malleable, you can simply take a piece of cloth and cut three horizontal holes in the center for the neck and arms to place over the doll. After it's on, cut and hem as you see fit. You can also take small strips of fabric and sew them around the arms and to the dress to act as sleeves. The same can be done with a shirt, pants, or overalls for a man.

Once dressed, cut the loop at the top and feed the wires through the dried apple head from the bottom. Once the head is in place at the shoulders, turn the wires down to curl over the head toward the back. At this point, you can focus on the face and hair of the doll, which will cover the wire stubs. I sometimes take some morning glory seeds and dab some honey on them and press them into the eye sockets. The same can be done with the mouth to form teeth—the seeds will just need to be painted white. (I rarely add teeth. Some doll makers do, but I think it makes them look a bit weird.) Sometimes I will substitute glass beads for the seeds, though.

Dolls can also be whittled or carved from wood and coal, depending on the maker's skill and experience. Other times dolls were made with crossed sticks tied together with a head of baked red clay or an apple. Many people still make rag dolls composed of cloth and stuffing, button eyes, and yarn hair. Dolls are also made from corn shucks: all you need to do is carve out a bit of the bottom, enough to slip personal concerns in, and seal it with wax. Paint a face and dress it by wrapping it in cloth to act as a dress or suit with a hat or bonnet, all of which is sewed around the cob. Just make sure that the shucked cob has dried in the sun for a couple of weeks so it doesn't mold.

One more note on the creation of a doll: Don't work on it while you're angry if your anger isn't toward the person the doll is for. Otherwise, you may imbue it with the personality of the person you're angry at, which will create a link to that person, thereby killing the purpose of the work. You should be as focused as possible on the person it is intended for. Even pricking your finger while sewing someone's doll could be detrimental to the working. If this happens, discard the needle and don't let any of your blood touch the doll. If the doll is for you, simply let your mind wander or say prayers while you work.

To work the doll baby, theoretically it has to be brought to life by naming and baptizing it. Fill a bowl with water, whiskey, or moonshine. Sometimes I will take the doll, covered in a white handkerchief, to the creek bed and baptize it there for certain cures or works. Get a white taper candle. Hold the doll before you, and with your right hand make the sign of the cross over it in the name of the Father, the Son, and the Holy Spirit while calling out the name of the person it is intended for: "I cross you with the name of [patient], in the name of the Father, the Son, and the Holy Spirit."

Next, light the candle and pass the doll over or through the flame from head to toe. Do so at a good pace and height so the doll doesn't burn. Pass it while saying, "I brand you by the name of [patient] and bring you to life as the bones of the desert were called up in the Word. In the name of the Father, the Son, and the Holy Spirit." Now take your bowl and hold the doll over it; dip the backs of your fingers in the water, and then barely shake your hand over the doll to sprinkle the water. Do so over its head, chest, and feet while saying, "I baptize you with the name of [person]. Anything done to you will be done to [person]. I call you up and tell you: Live! In the name of the Father, the Son, and the Holy Spirit, amen!"

If the doll is made of fabric or wood, you may dunk the doll into the water like a real baptism, doing so in the middle of the baptism prayer above. The act of baptizing dolls, charms, and other things is widespread in American folk magic, a layfolk adaptation from Christian doctrine and the supposed "new birth" that comes with the act.

After the baptism, if the doll is you, dress it with your cologne or perfume. A lot of people will see what they assume is a trick of the eyes. It often only occurs when you're not paying any mind, but sometimes the arms or legs of my dolls seem to twitch, smile, or "talk back"—especially if you're the one it's connected to, because there's a connection spelled between you.

Once the doll is baptized, you work with it by the intention of the spell. If you're binding a person to keep them from doing harm or to keep them behind you, blindfold the doll and wrap its limbs and body tightly with cords. If the person is a gossiper, sew the mouth shut, put duct tape over it, or pin it together. If you're calling a person home to you, bury the doll at the front door facedown with the head pointing toward the house; if the work is to uproot someone, take the doll to the crossroads and bury it with its head pointing away from your home's direction to "head on out."

If the doll is intended for healing, keep it in a safe, dry, and clean space and "work" the doll in intervals, either every Wednesday, Thursday, and Friday weekly, or simply once a week or once a month, by patting the doll on the chest and praying or talking to it, touching and praying over the part afflicted.

Once I came across an apple head doll online that was for sale by a woman who had found it in an old house in Virginia. The doll was very old, dressed as a man, and the hands were burned down to nubs. Obviously, someone with a good reason was very pissed off. I can only assume whoever it was intended for had sticky fingers.

If a doll made in your likeness is ever lost, you need to disassociate from it as much as possible: keep your nails clipped down, change the scent you wear, or cut your hair. One sure way that I've done is to go to a church altar alone. If there's some reason you can't do this, go anywhere a cross is erected—at a church outside, on the side of a road, or at a statue in a graveyard. Facing the cross, place a quarter facedown and stand on it with your right foot while making the famous hand form called the fig, where the hand is made into a fist with the thumb tucked between the index and middle finger. As you stand there, say, "The staff of Moses on my knee, the palm of Christ on my head, I am that I am, it's only I." Leave the quarter without looking back.

11

PRAY THE DEVIL DOWN
Folk Recipes and Remedies

You didn't think I'd leave you empty handed, did you? To end this work, I think it best to give tried-and-true works for you to gain an upper hand on life. Remember to heed the precautions when doing workings, employing spirits, and the like. This work can be dangerous for you and others when used carelessly.

RECIPES

Healing

- For general healing, write the names of the blessed family (Jesus, Mary, Joseph) on a piece of paper. Take a candle from a church and drip the wax on the paper while praying for the hand of Christ to be on the person needing healing. Fold the paper toward you and bind with a red string in the name of the Trinity. Carry it as close to the skin as possible.

- To protect from disease, wear a copper bracelet or ring.

- Fix a penny heads up to the bottom of a white taper candle and anoint it with blessed olive oil. If the person needing healing is present, place the tip in their navel and pray for the disease to be drawn out and into the candle. Hold the candle over their left shoulder and light it. Set it up on a plate covered with "silver paper" (foil) and let it burn down. When the candle has melted completely, have the person spit onto the wax, wrap it in the silver paper, and either bury it at the roots of a tree or in the corner of a crossroads.

• For burns, pass your hand over the burn, going away from the person or away from their heart. With each pass, say, "Three ladies came from the east, one with fire and two with frost. Out with the fire in with the frost! In the name of God the Father, God the Son, and God the Holy Spirit." Do this three times. Afterward, you and the person shouldn't light, make, or tend any fires until the next sunset passes. This includes cooking over a stove or using a lighter.

• Carry a walnut for rheumatism or arthritis—begin carrying it while it is still small and green. Once it is completely black and dry, toss it and replace it.

• Place their photo in the Bible facing Psalm 23 and pray over it. Leave it there for three days, then take it out and put it in a jar of clear water. Add dirt from a hospital or mountaintop, a tablespoon of lard, a pinch of tobacco, and a pinch of salt while praying for their well-being and health, calling on God and the ancestors to "wash their name," a term I heard Papaw use once when healing. Swirl the contents of the jar clockwise as the hand of the clock goes up to build up their strength and health, while still praying. Work this jar every Sunday until they are better. Once they are, drain the water at a crossroads and keep the strained contents; give these to the person in a bundle to hide in their home above their head. As long as it's there and stays dry, it'll keep their health up.

- For breathing issues, wear a "greened penny"—one that has oxidized, with a hole made through the chest of Abe.

Cleansing

- Pass a white candle over yourself or another from head to toe three times while saying the Lord's Prayer. Set the candle down and let it burn completely. Spit on the remains and bury it at a crossroads.

- Add to a bath of water 1 cup new blessed salt, 3 tablespoons white vinegar, and ½ cup hyssop. Take the bath before sunrise, washing downward only, while reciting Psalm 51:7. End the bath at sunrise and take a portion of the bathwater outside and cast the water toward the rising sun. To make blessed salt, simply pronounce the Lord's Prayer over it three times at sunrise, noon, and sunset. Do this for three consecutive days. The same is done with sweet oil for anointing. You can switch out ingredients with any of the following: a cap of tar water, a cap of ammonia, a strong cup of brewed coffee, a tablespoon of baking soda, or mud from a river after it has flooded (to further wash away your "debris")—just make sure to use an odd number of ingredients.

- Cut a lemon in half while holding two pennies (minted in the year of your birth) under your upper lip. Sprinkle a pinch of salt on each half, making an X, and insert the pennies in the center of each. Place the lemon under your bed to sleep over for three days, namely Wednesday, Thursday, and Friday. Remove the lemon and bury it off property on Saturday.

- To remove conjugation or ill luck, wash your current change of clothes with salt and vinegar and then burn them. Take the ashes to a crossroads at midnight and scatter them when the wind blows. Leave without looking back and go a different way home then you came. For this I recommend going to a crossroads far from your home.

Protection

- For protection during travel, carry a rabbit's foot or a jack containing nine yarrow leaves, three pennies, and dust from the home.

- To protect from the evil eye, get some red yarn and go to the oldest grave in a cemetery. Walk counterclockwise around it seven times while wrapping the yarn around your left wrist once for every turn while praying Psalm 23. You can also wear gold or silver, or embroider an *X* in the left-leg hem of your underwear. Don't forget to leave an offering for the grave in return for you doing the work there.

- To protect from being conjured, carry in a sack a horseshoe nail, ground ivy root, and blessed salt. You can also sprinkle a mixture of salt, black pepper, and red pepper in your shoes or wear a silver dime on your right ankle.

- To protect from illness, wear a bag of asafoetida, salt, and a copper penny.

- Wear a rosary, cross, or other religious symbol.

- To guard against roaming ghosts and other haints, my family would always get five sticks and bind them in such a way as to make a five-pointed star, called a "witch's mark" in Appalachia.

You can still see these stars hung on the sides of homes and barns everywhere.

Court and Law

- Take a silver spoon and gather dirt from the grave of a baby (because they've never been convicted of anything) and leave nine pennies behind in its place. Mix the dirt with sugar, cinnamon, and flour. Make a packet of brown paper with your name written on it and the name of the courthouse below that. Mark out all consonants so both resonate with their vowels. Carry the packet in your left shoe to keep the judge on your side.

- To keep the law away, make a sachet with an Indian-head penny, tobacco, and moss from the foundation of a church. Bless it following the method given previously to keep all law enforcement far from you.

- Carry items for good luck when going to court, such as a peep-stone, four-leaf clover, etc. You can also sprinkle new salt in your shoes to make you "slicker than glass" so you'll get by just fine. According to my mother, you should also take a toothbrush and a change of solid white clothes. This prevents you from going to jail because you're already prepared.

Love and Lust

- Take two pieces of paper and write each person's name on them with their date of birth. Bind them together with red string and dust it with a mixture of powdered rose petals, flour, and sugar. Bury the bundle on the east side of a tree, preferably a willow, to bring them together.

- To keep a lover from running around, make a sachet of mayapple root, rose petals, and bloodroot. Include some connection to them: dirty garments, hair, nails, or a photo. Bind it with a red string. Bless the sachet and bury it under the doorstep. Every time the lover walks over it, it'll keep them faithful. To "feed" the work, water it with your first morning urine once a month while calling their name out three times and telling them to stay as the River Jordan did.

- For new love, give them wine or whiskey in which you've soaked your toenails for three days, from Wednesday to Friday. Strain it on Saturday morning. This will win over anyone.

- To have a lover return, whisper their name when you wake up and when you go to bed for nine days. On the tenth day, cast three handfuls of salt into the fireplace and recite the following for each: "I charm you on your breast and sides, as the colt follows the mare; as the rain seeks the earth; seek and find me. By the voice that called the Virgin, I call you back to me."

- To have one fall in love with you, take a cloth, shirt, or other garment for them to wear. Wet it with your first morning's urine for three days. Then find two coupling animals (rooting snakes, mating dogs, etc.) and cover them with the cloth and then take it back. Give it to your lover to wear. Of course you can mask any possible smell with your preferred cologne or perfume.

- To incite passion in a relationship, hide a turkey bone wrapped and tied in their unwashed garments under the bed. Take a "stray hair" from their head and one from your own; bundle them in a bag with honeysuckle blooms, sugar, and ground hard candy; hang this on the bedpost.

Money and Gambling

- For sports, take a dish that was broken by accident and make three cuts on the chest and four the back. Powder some dandelion root really fine and rub into the cuts. This is supposed to "toughen up" the person and bring success.

- Bake the tip of a cow tongue. Take it to seven cemeteries and touch it to the oldest headstone in each yard, leaving a dime for each grave. Place the tongue in your mouth over your own and say your prayers for success in money or gambling. Carry in the left pocket.

- On a full moon, take the left hind foot of a white rabbit to the oldest grave at midnight. At the headstone, pour some moonshine for the spirit of the grave, telling them to help you witch the foot under the eyes of the Trinity. Dip the toes of the foot in the same moonshine and trace the engraved dates on the headstone with the toes while saying, "As many days are here inscribed, the same for me will be lucky and safe." Do this three times, then leave the rest of the moonshine and exit the graveyard following the precautions spoken of before.

Uprooting

- To get someone to leave town or move away from your area, take a splinter of lightning-struck wood and place it under their porch steps or where they'll walk over it.

- Alternatively, take dirt from their footstep or where they recently walked and fold it up in a brown paper bag. Dunk it in water and then burn it while saying, "Water and fire are at your feet. By the voice that chased Adam from the garden, get gone." Repeat until it is ashes. Take those ashes and mix them

with dirt from their yard and sprinkle it where they'll walk.
To sprinkle it, walk backward an odd number of steps while
saying their name and repeating the above.

- Powder some dead spiders and mix with black pepper and salt.
Sprinkle this in an *X* formation where the person will walk
over it.

- Take a spool of handspun yarn and pierce it with thirteen
needles. Relieve yourself on it while saying the person's name
and telling them to leave. Bury this where they will walk over
it.

Gossip

- To stop gossip, take a photo of the person responsible and cut
out their eyes so they cannot "give the eye" and cut out the
mouth so they cannot "speak the eye." Place this in a mason
jar and piss on it while calling their name, praying for their
tongue to draw, for salt and vinegar to be in their mouth. Add
nine pins and needles. Every day for nine days, tap the top with
a silver spoon while praying your petition. On the tenth day,
bury the jar in a churchyard or cemetery.

- An old trick for this is to "catch their voice": get a string
and begin to tie a knot in it. Call for them when you're
around them, and when they answer, without them knowing, pull the knot tight. The more knots you can get before
they come, the stronger the spell will be. Take the cord and
place it in a bottle filled with vinegar, alum, red dust, and
your first morning urine. Shake the bottle while praying for
them to stop.

For Success/To Turn Your Luck Around

- Catch your first urine in the morning in a jar and add a handful of salt to the liquid. Take it and walk nine steps out and away from your home. At the ninth step, stop and recite the Lord's Prayer, following it with a prayer for your luck to turn around and for all ill fortune to be chased off by the Holy Trinity. Take a step backward toward the house and do the same. Do so for each step, counting nine in reverse. At the doorstep, turn toward the house and wash the doorstep with the mixture in the jar and without looking back, go back inside and think nothing more of it.

- Sprinkle new salt in your shoes and you'll be "slicker than a slug" or "slicker than glass" in everything you set out to do.

REMEDIES

Burns

- Wave your hand over the burn going away from the person while reciting, "Two angels came and sat on a stone; one with fire and one with frost. Go away fire, come in frost! In the name of the Father, the Son, and the Holy Spirit." Recite it three times, passing the hand for each, followed by a breath blown on the burn directed away from the person.

- Light a candle used during a wake or funeral and set it on the burn. Turn a clear glass over it to encompass the candle. When the flame goes out, fill the glass with water and pour this over the burn. What harmed you can cure you.

Swelling

- Wash the place with well water, stumpwater, or rainwater from Easter Sunday.

- Wrap the limb with a strip of eel skin while saying the Lord's Prayer and a Hail Mary.

Fever

- Mama always said, "feed a cold, starve a fever." Don't eat anything once the fever comes on. Wipe yourself down with an ice-cold washcloth while reciting the Lord's Prayer three times. Once the cloth is no longer cold, wring the water into a bowl and throw the cloth into the freezer. Place the bowl under the bed or couch and lay over it until the fever breaks.

- Wear dirt collected from a church on St. John's Day in a bag about the neck.

Nightmares and Insomnia

- Make a sachet containing three lamb's ears leaves, nine blackberry leaves harvested before September 29, and blessed salt. Sleep with this around the neck or under the pillow.

- Sleep with a rabbit's left hind foot under the mattress.

- Sleep under an authentic dream catcher, but never touch the feathers or the charm will be ineffective.

Bedwetting and Sleepwalking

- For bed wetting, as previously mentioned, give a tea made from corn silk. Sweeten to taste.

- Place a Bible beneath the bed while saying, "In the name of the Father, the Son, and the Holy Spirit, as the waters of Jordan stood so shall the waters of [name]."

- For sleepwalking, place a Bible at the head of the bed and a bucket of water at the foot.

- Alternatively, take one of the person's shirts and tie a knot in it. Place it lengthwise on the foot of the bed at their feet so they will stay sleeping.

Sores/Wounds

- For sore hands or feet, soak them in vinegar, salt, and warm water for thirty minutes.

- Let a dog lick the sores or wounds and they'll be healed in three days, as they were for Lazarus in the Bible.

- Rub the wound good with salt and honey and then wash it in warm water.

Toothache

- Carry the boiled and dried tip of a cow's tongue around the neck.

- Drink water from a cobalt blue glass.

- Chew the grass that grows on a newly dug grave on a Sunday.

- Wear a deer, hog, or buffalo tooth around the neck.

- Wear a rosary.

- Take the jawbone of a donkey and walk backward nine steps, then drop the bone there and leave it. This is preferably done somewhere you'll never see the bone again.

EPILOGUE

Well, here we are. At the end. This book has been tough to write. I've been ragged with decisions and hesitations. When I first decided to write this book, I had no idea the emotional impact it would have on me. Now that I'm writing the end, I wonder, Did I tell too much? What will this information be put to use for truly? Have I made a mistake and forsaken something? These questions have racked my skull from one end of Tennessee to the other.

My hope is that I have done my best to organize this book in a way to introduce you to this folk practice for you, as layfolk, to effectively put the roots of this land to use. I've led you through the culture, through stories of the hills and my own family, and down paths of superstition, through the graveyards and churches. We've dug our feet into the dirt, and spoke with the Unseen.

For so long this practice has been clutched to my chest, with the memories of my grandfathers and grandmothers, stuck on autumn pumpkin pies and summer fishing trips. Appalachian folks are sentimental, close-knit, resourceful people. We don't shun outsiders, but we also won't tear down the fence between us and them. In writing this book, I'm giving something up that is tied to my bones. I bared my blood and soul to write these pages. I've sat at the altar to my ancestors in silence, wondering what they would do. I've sat in the rain and dug my toes into the red clay dirt, asking if sharing this was the right thing to do.

Writing this book brought me back to childhood memories that at first seemed to have no connection to this work, but on further reflection are a critical part of it. When I was five years old, I tripped getting onto the back porch of my great-grandfather's house while carrying a mason jar of caterpillars. The jar shattered and my knees were cut up, but Mamaw Margie patched me up with some peroxide and bandages. No folk remedies or anything. Another time, when I was about the same age, Mama and Daddy took us down to Pigeon Forge for the weekend, where we stayed in a cheap motel with an indoor pool. We had so much fun, and it's one of the only good memories when the whole family was happy. I guess we were, but I was too young to tell otherwise—and I don't care to learn otherwise.

The clearest memory of my Papaw Trivett was when we arrived one day and he was sitting on the couch and right away said, "There's my Peanut!" His funeral was the only time I've seen my Nana cry (aside from allergies) while they did the twenty-one-gun salute.

I also remembered again and again the times my Mamaw Hopson would make biscuits for an army, intended for just my sister and me. I remembered so much, I went in the kitchen and worked dough just to remember more through the scent and feel of flour everywhere and the dough sticking to my hands. I even went to a store and stood in front of the wind chimes, thinking about how many she kept on the porch and in the kitchen's floor-to-ceiling window that looked out to the barn and the bridge that covered the creek.

None of these things had anything to do with roots, charms, or cures. I don't know who or what, but *something* pulled me down those memory lanes and kept pulling me until I learned how it was connected. All those childhood memories had nothing to do with this, yet they represent everything held in this practice. I wasn't remembering cures and charms or techniques for a reason: they *weren't* everything. I was reminded about the love and soul of my family, the blood that binds us and takes us back in time. I was reminded of my family's utmost faith in God and the strength that gave them in their bones.

There's a unified spirit to this practice that I can't identify as anything else other than *Appalachia*. A song by Jeff Brown & Still Lonesome called "Appalachia Is My Name" sums this up well. Appalachia is much more than sweet tea, gentle grannies, and fresh apple pies. There are criminals who will show their teeth at you to get what they want. Trust me, that ain't a smile. And there are folks so caught up in their drug addiction that no amount of prayer could keep them from the grave.

Many people do what they can to survive. Even that statement doesn't cover the woes some of us go through. There have been times the fridge was bone-dry because we needed to sell the food stamps to help make rent or keep the power on. Lots of us can't afford to pay for health insurance or to go to the doctor for a potential emergency. These mountains give us strength, but they can also turn you lonesome and mad. I can see why some turn to the bottle.

These mountains can bring you to salvation or walk you to death in the dark. There's a lot of bad blood in these hills. It hollers amen in the church, sits at the kitchen table talking about what so and so did, and swims inside the bottle of 'shine. Paired with the struggle, it is the magic and medicine that has kept us up and going. The church is a steady hand in a lot of this work. Even though many people in Appalachia aren't churchgoing folk, they still have their faith, which is evident in almost every formula. As Nana always said, "You can get saved talking to God while sitting on the john just the same as you could at the altar."

We have our own way of faith, food, dress, music, and magic. We have our own lands and hills and trails . . . and it's all ours, all that we can see. We may not be proud of some things, but that doesn't mean we'll divorce it. From our struggles and problems to our faith and culture, this is Appalachia. We are Appalachia.

This culture relied on folk magic and medicine for centuries, when nary a doctor or preacher could be found. It lifted and placed curses, healed wounds inside and out, gave faith and hope to people, and, most importantly, endured. But this tradition is at a crossroads: live on or pass on. Either this work continues and lives, or it gets forgotten and breaks down more over time with each passing generation until the heirs of Appalachia have never seen the magic and faith of their forefolks.

This is poor man's work: tins cans, wading in the creeks, plugging trees, and plowing the fields. It demands you work and sacrifice blood and sweat until you're bone-tired for it. Didn't you hear? Faith without works is dead. I have faith that this work will continue, respected and honored, inside and outside of Appalachia. I may come from a broken home, bad blood, and poverty; I may never go to college, own my own big home, or travel the world; but I will have these mountains to hold my spirit, support my feet when they're old and stumbling, and make a bed for me when I give up the ghost.

When everything's said and done, I'll still be here drying cobs in the sun, gathering herbs in the woods, and moss from the creeks with that rabbit's foot in my pocket; I'll be there bartering with farmers for milk and wool and hair. I think the most important thing for any tradition to truly live on in its culture of birth is to have honest folks to represent it and pass it on. Some things will follow me to the grave. Times are changing, and a lot of this tradition's purposes and needs are fading from society as Appalachia outgrows its "primitive" and "redneck" ways.

Amidst this progression, I will be here in the backwoods when needed and sought, curing with silver and boiled milk, speaking to unseen guests, and spelling folks' history through dead man's eyes until the day I die. The things I'll take to the grave with me? Well, they're better left between the Devil and me, whispered only from my grave to those with the gift, heart, and spirit to hold it.

BIBLIOGRAPHY

Allen, David E., and Gabrielle Hatfield. *Medicinal Plants in Folk Tradition: An Ethnobotany of Britain & Ireland*. Portland, OR: Timber Press, 2004.

Bierhorst, John, ed. *The Deetkatoo: Native American Stories About Little People*. New York: Marrow Junior Books, 1998.

Blaustein, Richard. *The Thistle and the Brier: Historical Links and Cultural Parallels Between Scotland and Appalachia*. Jefferson, NC: McFarland, 2003.

Boyle, Virginia Frazer. *Devil Tales*. New York: Harper & Brothers, 1900.

Burdick, Lewis Dayton. *Magic and Husbandry: The Folklore of Agriculture*. Binghampton, NY: Otseningo Publishing Co., 1905.

Campbell, John. *Witchcraft and Second Sight in the Highlands and Islands of Scotland: Tales and Traditions Collected Entirely from Oral Sources*. Detroit: Sing Tree Press, 1970.

Cavender, Anthony. *Folk Medicine in Appalachia*. Chapel Hill: University of North Carolina Press, 2007.

Chadwell, Tyler J., and Tiffany D. Martin. "Mountain Mystics: Magic Practitioners in Appalachian Witchlore." *Bulletin of the Transilvania University of Brasov, Series IV: Philology & Cultural Studies*, no. 1 (September 2016): 49–56.

Cross, Tom Peete. "Witchcraft in North Carolina," *Studies in Philology* XVI, no. 3 (July 1919): 217–287.

Drake, Richard B. *A History of Appalachia*. Lexington: University of Kentucky Press, 2001.

Dunwich, Gerina. *Herbal Magick: A Witch's Guide to Herbal Folklore and Enchantments*. Franklin Lakes, NJ: Career Press, 2002.

Dykeman, Wilma. "Appalachian Mountains." In *Encyclopaedia Britannica.* Accessed July 1, 2017. *http://www.britannica.com/place/Appalachian -Mountains.*

Ehle, John. *Trail of Tears: The Rise and Fall of the Cherokee Nation.* New York: Anchor Books, 1989.

Gainer, Patrick W. *Witches, Ghosts, and Signs: Folklore of the Southern Appalachians.* Morgantown: West Virginia University Press, 2008.

Gary, Gemma. *The Black Toad: West Country Witchcraft and Magic.* New York: Troy Books, 2016.

Gutch, Mrs. Eliza, and Mabel Peacock. "Examples of Printed Folk-Lore Concerning Lincolnshire." *County Folk-Lore,* vol. 5. Publications of the Folk-Lore Society, vol. 63. London: David Nutt, 1908.

Hohman, John George. *Pow-Wows or Long Lost Friend: A Collection of Mysterious and Invaluable Arts and Remedies.* Pomeroy, WA: Health Research, 1971. Reprint.

Hyatt, Harry Middleton. *Hoodoo – Conjuration – Witchcraft – Rootwork.* 5 vols. Hannibal, MO: Western Publishing, 1970.

Jones, Kelvin I. *Joan the Crone: The History and Craft of the Cornish Witch.* Norwich, UK: Oakmagic Publications, 1999.

Jones, Loyal. *Faith and Meaning in the Southern Uplands.* Urbana: University of Illinois Press, 1999.

Kilpatrick, Jack Frederick, ed. *The Wahnenauhi Manuscript: Historical Sketches of the Cherokees Together with Some of Their Customs, Traditions, and Superstitions* Smithsonian Bureau of Ethnology.

Knightly, Charles. *The Perpetual Almanack of Folklore.* London: Thames and Hudson, 1987. Reprinted 1994.

Lane, Megan. "Hoodoo Heritage: A Brief History of American Folk Religion." Bachelor's thesis, University of Georgia, 2005. Accessed September 23, 2017. *https://getd.libs.uga.edu/pdfs/lane_megan_e_200805_ma.pdf.*

Lavator, Ludwig. *Of Ghostes and Spirites, Walking by Night.* Translated by R. H. London: Thomas Creede, 1596,

Milnes, Gerald C. *Signs, Cures, and Witchery: German Appalachian Folklore.* Knoxville: University of Tennessee Press, 2007.

Mooney, James. *Myths of the Cherokee: Extract from the Nineteenth Annual Report of the Bureau of American Ethnology.* Washington, DC: Government Printing Office, 1902.

———. "The Swimmer Manuscript: Cherokee Sacred Formulas and Medicinal Prescriptions." *Bureau of American Ethnology Bulletin* 99 (1932): 1–319.

Owen, J. J. *Our Little Doctor: Helen Craib-Beighle and the Magic Power of Her Electric Hand.* San Francisco: Hicks-Judd Co., 1893.

Panati, Charles. *Extraordinary Origins of Everyday Things.* New York: HarperCollins, 1989.

Pickering, David. *Cassell Dictionary of Superstitions.* N.p.: Cassell, 1996.

Price, Charles E. *Haints, Witches, and Boogers: Tales from Upper East Tennessee.* Winston-Salem: John F. Blair Press, 1992.

Randolph, Vance. *Ozarks Superstitions.* New York: Columbia University Press, 1947.

Rice, John R. *The Power of Pentecost: Or the Fullness of the Spirit.* Murfreesboro, TN: Sword of the Lord Publishers, 1949.

Richard, Chase. *American Folk Tales and Songs.* New York: Dover Publications, 1971.

Roper, Jonathan, ed. *Charms, Charmers and Charming.* New York: Palgrave Macmillan, 2009.

Schwartz, Alvin. *Cross Your Fingers, Spit in Your Hat.* Philadelphia and New York: J. B. Lippincott Company, 1974.

Snedden, Andrew. *Witchcraft and Magic in Ireland.* Basingstoke, UK: Palgrave Macmillan, 2015.

Thacker, Larry. *Mountain Mysteries: The Mystic Traditions of Appalachia.* Johnson City, TN: Overmountain Press, 2007.

Wigginton, Eliot. *The Foxfire Book.* 11 vols. Garden City, NY: Anchor Books, 1972.

Wood, J. Maxwell. *Witchcraft and Superstitious Record: In the South-Western District of Scotland.* Dumfries, Scotland: J. Maxwell & Son, 1911.

Yeats, W. B. *Fairy and Folk Tales of the Irish Peasantry.* New York: Courier Corporation, 1888.

ABOUT THE AUTHOR

Jake Richard's family heritage in Appalachia goes back generations. Known by some folks as Old Buck or Kudzu, Jake has practiced folk magic for almost a decade and teaches classes on folk healing, ancestor veneration, and divination. He writes about these topics on his blog, Holy Stones and Iron Bones, and owns Little Chicago Conjure, a supplier of Appalachian folk magic supplies and ingredients.

TO OUR READERS

Weiser Books, an imprint of Red Wheel/Weiser, publishes books across the entire spectrum of occult, esoteric, speculative, and New Age subjects. Our mission is to publish quality books that will make a difference in people's lives without advocating any one particular path or field of study. We value the integrity, originality, and depth of knowledge of our authors.

Our readers are our most important resource, and we appreciate your input, suggestions, and ideas about what you would like to see published.

Visit our website at *www.redwheelweiser.com* to learn about our upcoming books and free downloads, and be sure to go to *www.redwheelweiser.com/newsletter* to sign up for newsletters and exclusive offers.

You can also contact us at *info@rwwbooks.com* or at

Red Wheel/Weiser, LLC
65 Parker Street, Suite 7
Newburyport, MA 01950